Daily Discoveries for June

Thematic Learning Activities for **EVERY DAY**

Written by Elizabeth Cole Midgley

Illustrated by Jennette Guymon-King

Teaching & Learning Company

1204 Buchanan St., P.O. Box 10
Carthage, IL 62321-0010

This book belongs to

____

Several of the activities in this book involve preparing, tasting and sharing food items. We urge you to be aware of any food allergies or restrictions your students may have and to supervise these activities diligently. All food-related suggestions are identified with this allergy-alert symbol: ⚠

Please note: small food items (candies, raisins, cereal, etc.) can also pose a choking hazard.

Cover art by Jennette Guymon-King

Table of Contents

Dear Teacher or Parent,

Due to the stimulus of a high-tech world, parents and teachers are often faced with the challenge of how to capture the attention of a child and create an atmosphere of meaningful learning opportunities. Often we search for new ways to meet this challenge and help young people transfer their knowledge, skills and experiences from one area to another. Subjects taught in isolation can leave a feeling of fragmentation. More and more educators are looking for ways to be able to integrate curriculum so that their students can fully understand how things relate to each other.

The Daily Discoveries series has been developed to that end. The premise behind this series has been, in part, the author's educational philosophy: anything can be taught and absorbed by others in a meaningful way, depending upon its presentation.

In this series, each day has been researched around the history of a specific individual or event and has been developed into a celebration or theme with integrated curriculum areas. In this approach to learning students draw from their own experience and understanding of things, to a level of processing new information and skills.

The Daily Discoveries series is an almanac-of-sorts, 12 books (one for each month) that present a thematically based curriculum for grades K-6. The series contains hundreds and hundreds of resources and ideas that can be a natural springboard to learning. These ideas have been used in the classroom and at home, and are fun as well as educationally sound. The activities have been endorsed by professors, teachers, parents and, best of all, by children.

The Daily Discoveries series can be used in the following ways for school or home:
* to develop new skills and reinforce previous learning
* to create a sense of fun and celebration every day
* as tutoring resources
* as enrichment activities that can be used as time allows
* for family fun activities

Sincerely,

Elizabeth

Elizabeth Cole Midgley

Kentucky and Tennessee Statehood Day

June 1

Setting the Stage

- Ask a travel agency for posters, brochures and travel information about Kentucky and Tennessee to display with related literature.

- Construct a semantic web with words your students think of when you say the words *Kentucky* and *Tennessee*.

- Cut out shapes of Kentucky and Tennessee and mount them on a wall. Let students cut pictures from magazines to illustrate features of each state and glue them on the shapes. (Examples: Kentucky—horses, KFC™, bluegrass; Tennessee—country music, Elvis)

Historical Background

Kentucky and Tennessee gained statehood as the 15th and 16th states on this day. Kentucky became a state in 1792 and four years later, Tennessee became a state in 1796. At that time, both states were considered frontier areas. Daniel Boone led settlers into Kentucky in 1750. Andrew Jackson was part of the first group to go to the settlement of Nashville, Tennessee, in 1788. The settling of these two states was the beginning of westward expansion, though they are no longer considered the west.

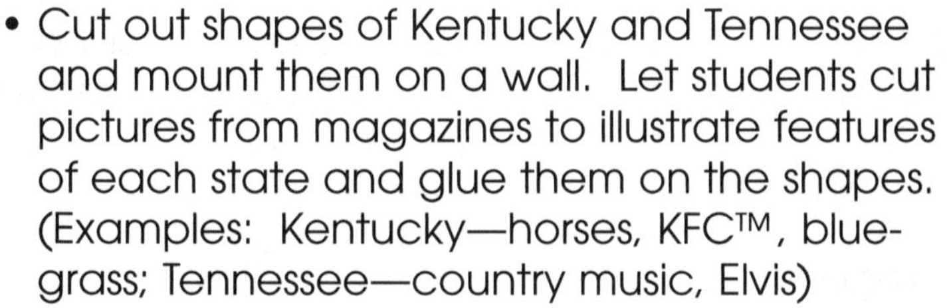

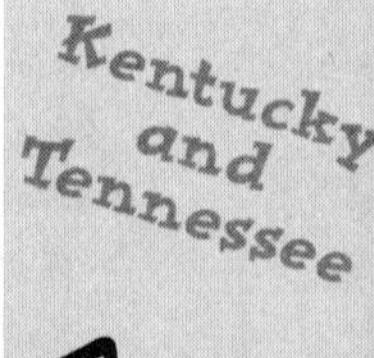

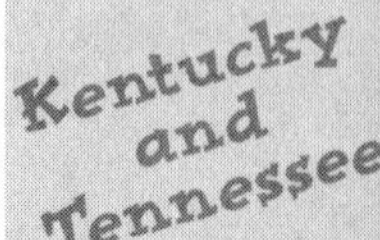

Literary Exploration

America the Beautiful, Kentucky by Sylvia McNair
A Historical Album of Kentucky by Adam Smith
Kentucky by Allan Carpenter
Kentucky by Dennis B. Fradin
Kentucky by Kathleen Thompson
Kentucky in Words and Pictures by Dennis B. Fradin
The Southeast: Georgia, Kentucky, Tennessee by Thomas G. Aylesworth
Tennessee by Allan Carpenter
Tennessee by Kathleen Thompson
Tennessee in Words and Pictures by Dennis B. Fradin
Tennessee Trailblazers by Pat McKissack

Language Experience

- Create a Venn diagram depicting the similarities and differences between the states of Kentucky and Tennessee.

- Point out to students the double letters in *Tennessee*. How many other state names can they think of that have double letters in them? (Example: Minnesota) Do any other state names have three sets of double letters? (Mississippi)

- Have students research to discover where Kentucky and Tennessee got their names. They can report their findings to the rest of the class.

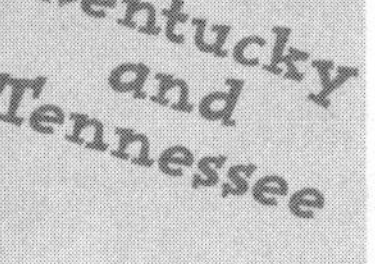

Writing Experience

- Chirculissa, near Memphis, Tennessee, is a reconstructed Choctaw Indian Village dating from the 1500s. Challenge students to imagine how these early people lived. Have them write diary entries from the viewpoint of Choctaw girls and boys in that long ago village.

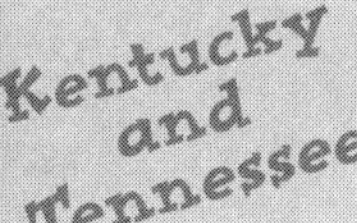

Writing Experience continued

- Let students imagine they are famous country singers from Nashville, Tennessee, doing concerts around the country. Have them write about their imaginary adventures.

- Have students create travel brochures about Kentucky or Tennessee, describing them so that other people will want to go visit there. See page 8 for art ideas.

- Students can write acrostic poems about Kentucky and Tennessee. Have them print the name of one of the states down the left side of a sheet of paper. Then they can come up with descriptive words or things or people from the state that begin with those letters. (Examples: K— E— N— T—Thoroughbred horses, U— C—Churchill Downs racetrack, K—KFC™, Y)

Math Experience

- Have students research Kentucky and Tennessee facts, then use the information to create math problems for the class to solve. They can make problems comparing the two states' populations or sizes as well as their average summer or winter temperatures. Then let them present their problems to the class to solve.

Science/Health Experience

- Study the kinds of plants, trees and flowers that grow in Kentucky and Tennessee. What is the climate like? Is it good for growing plants? How long is the growing season?

Social Studies Experience

- Study the states of Kentucky and Tennessee and find out what makes each one a unique state.

- Ask students which states border Kentucky and Tennessee on the north, south, east and west. Look on a map to check their answers.

Music/Dramatic Experience

• Listen to some country music. Let students who are fans of country music bring their favorite cassettes or CDs to play for everyone.

• Students can try making "hillbilly" music by blowing tunes on ceramic jugs, clacking spoons together and slapping their legs.

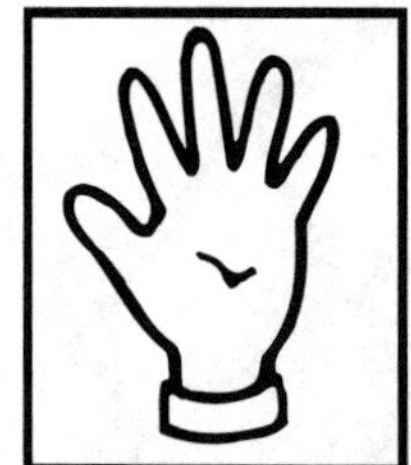

Physical/Sensory Experience

• Invite a dance instructor to teach your class basic folk dancing.

Arts/Crafts Experience

• Students can draw illustrations to go with their Kentucky or Tennessee travel brochures, showing the natural beauty of the state and some of its famous features or landmarks.

• Horses are a major attraction in both Kentucky and Tennessee. Have students try drawing horses of various kinds.

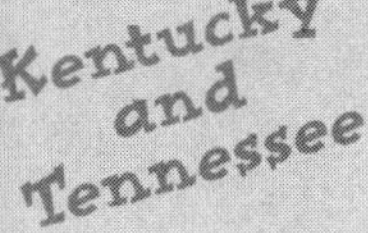

Extension Activities

• Stage a "Grand Old Opry" like the one in Nashville, Tennessee. Students can dress up in "country" outfits and lip sync favorite country songs and perform country dances.

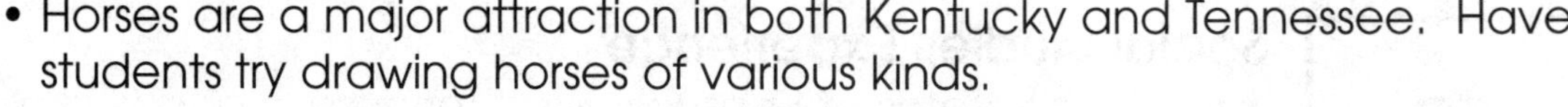

Teacher Appreciation Day

June 2

Setting the Stage

- To show appreciation for the teacher today, students can make a special bulletin board. They can each draw a full-length self-portrait, then another picture of something they really enjoyed learning this year (science experiment, favorite book, etc.). Both pictures can be cut out and pinned on the bulletin board with the caption: "Our Bodies Grew and Our Minds Grew."

- Students can draw summer activities they will soon be involved in. Mount them on a bulletin board with the caption: "How many days until . . ." At the bottom of the bulletin board, print: *Just _____ Days* (with a daily countdown of how many days are left until school is out).

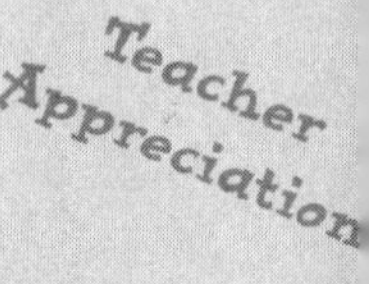

- Rather than have students write their appreciation in cards or letters, let them write "graffiti" notes. Although graffiti is normally unacceptable, they can write on a mock fence which you have made of brown butcher paper (complete with knotholes and imperfections). Mount it on a wall. As students think of something to write, they can write their thank-yous to the teacher on the fence.

- Construct a semantic web with words your students think of when you say the word *teacher*.

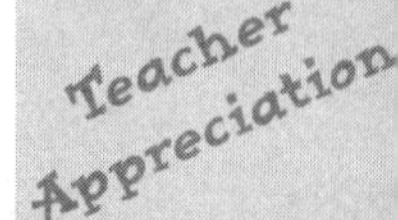

Literary Exploration

Arthur's Teacher Trouble by Marc Brown
The Best Teacher in the World by Bernice Chardiet
I Can Be a Teacher by Beatrice Beckman
A Hippopotamus Ate the Teacher by Mike Thaler
The Teacher from the Black Lagoon by Mike Thaler

Language Experience

• Give each student a worksheet with reading or grammatical errors all over the page. Let students correct the work like you correct theirs!

• How many words can your students come up with that rhyme with the word *teach*?

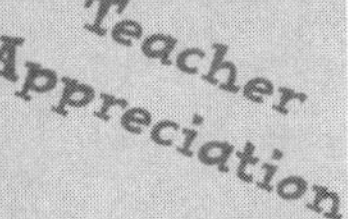

Writing Experience

• Have students each write about a former influential teacher or describe what an ideal teacher would be for them. See reproducible on page 13.

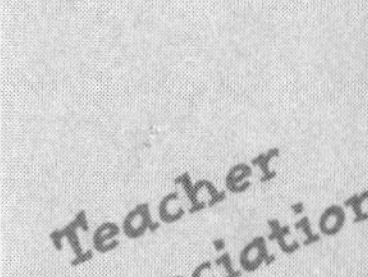

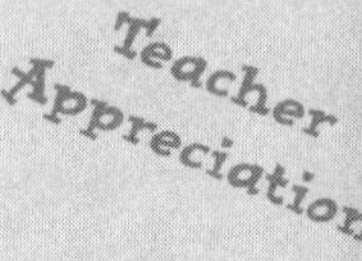

Math Experience

• Pair students up and let them take on the role of "teacher" and student. One student does half of the assigned math problems and the other corrects the work. Then they switch roles.

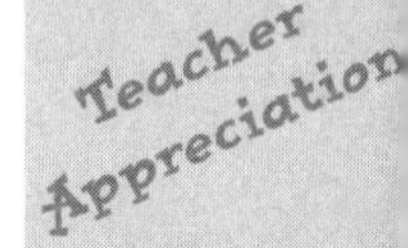

Science/Health Experience

* Let students take turns playing "teacher" sharing with the class all they learned on a given subject in a science or a health-related subject this year.

Social Studies Experience

* Let students play "teacher," sharing their knowledge on social studies-related topics.

Music/Dramatic Experience

* Let students' role-play at a dress-up center what it would be like to be a teacher. It may be revealing to hear your students "talk" like you.

Extension Activities

* Let your students give you report cards to "grade" you as a teacher (for kindness, expectations, preparation, teaching strategies, listening ability, presentation of topics, etc). This will tell you if you "made the grade" with your students!

Values Education Experience

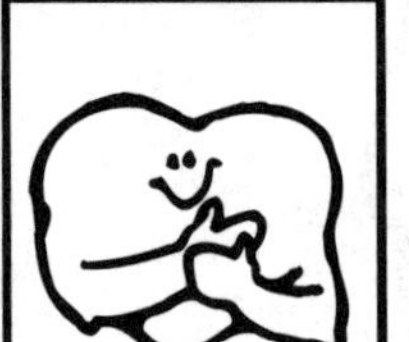

* Express to your students the value it is for you to be their teacher, watching them learn and progress throughout the school year. Thank them for their encouragement or enthusiasm.

Teachers

Soccer Day

June 3

Setting the Stage
- Display students' work next to a picture of a soccer ball with the caption: "We're Using Our Head!"

Literary Exploration
Berenstain Bears' Soccer Star by Stan Berenstain
Dulcie Dando, Soccer Star by Sue Stops
Dylan's Day Out by Peter Catalanotto
Great Game of Soccer by Howard Liss
Illustrated Soccer Dictionary for Young People by James Gardner
Jerry on the Line by Brenda Seabrooke
Old Turtle's Soccer Team by Leonard Kessler
Shot from Midfield by Tommy Hallowell
Soccer by Bert Rosenthal
Soccer by Jack Scagnetti
Soccer by Clive Toye
Soccer Basics by Alex Yannis
Soccer Sam by Jean Marzollo
Soccer Techniques in Pictures by Michael Brown
Soccer: The Game and How to Play It by Gary Rosenthal
S.O.R. Losers by Avi

Writing Experience

• Let students write about why they enjoy the game of soccer. See reproducible on page 18.

• Have students imagine they are each a soccer ball. They can describe a game from the balls' viewpoint. Encourage them to write with imagination and humor.

Math Experience

• Duplicate the soccer ball patterns on page 19 for students. On the center black section of the soccer ball they write an answer with white crayon or chalk. On the white sections of the ball, they write math problems with that answer (Example: If the black section says 10, the white sections can be 5 + 5, and 4 + 6, and so on.)

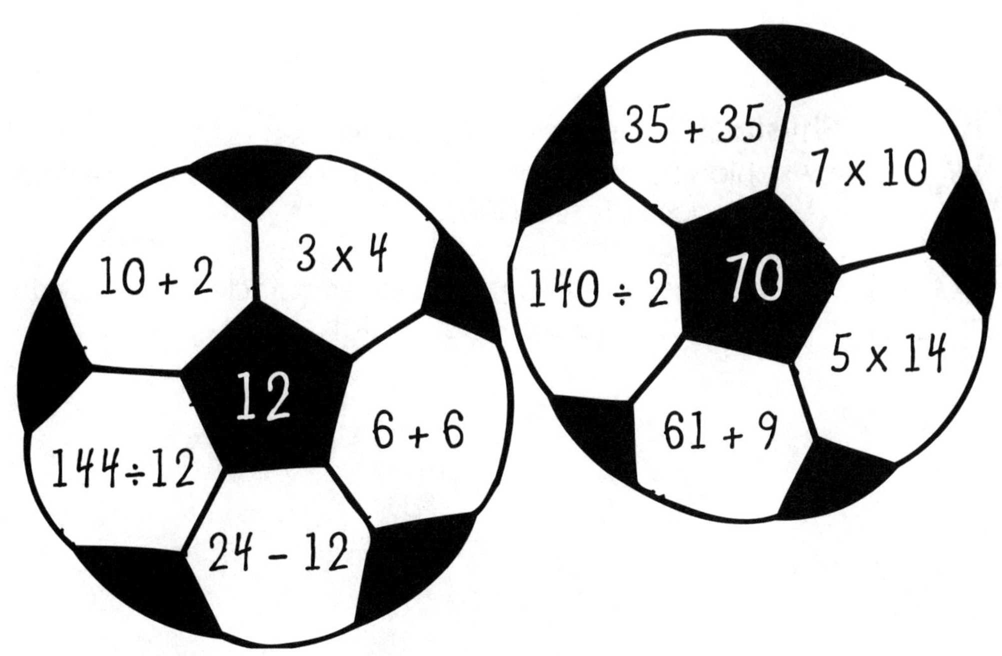

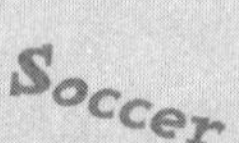

Science/Health Experience

• Review soccer safety.

• Discuss the value of regular exercise, playing soccer or another sport, biking, jogging, etc. Ask students to share what they do for exercise. Talk about what happens to the body when we don't exercise enough.

Social Studies Experience

• Find out about the areas of the world where soccer is played. Have students locate them on a world map.

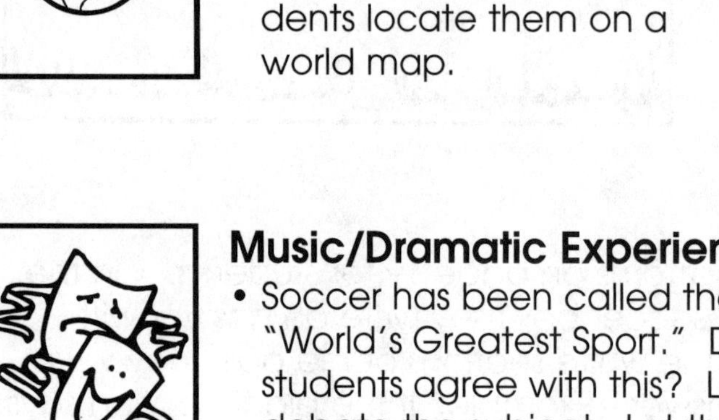

Music/Dramatic Experience

• Soccer has been called the "World's Greatest Sport." Do your students agree with this? Let them debate the subject. Let those who disagree suggest which sport they think should be given that title.

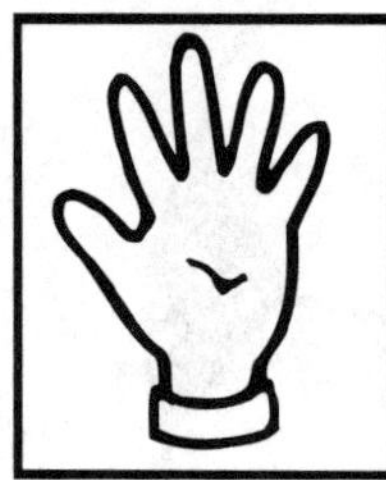

Physical/Sensory Experience

• Ask high school soccer team members to come and teach your class basic soccer techniques.

• As weather permits, play soccer outside today, perhaps challenging another class to a soccer match.

Arts/Crafts Experience
• Let students make papier-mâché soccer balls.

Extension Activities
• Invite an experienced soccer player to come and talk to your class about the game.

⚠ Serve miniature Skor™ candy bars for a treat.

Follow-Up/Homework Idea
• Encourage students to practice their soccer skills after school for some good exercise.

I get a kick out of...

Good-Bye School Day

June 4
(varies)

Setting the Stage

- Let students draw self-portraits and cut around the shapes. They can write about their favorite thing from this school year on drawing paper. Then have them cut around the writing in the shape of speech balloons (as in cartoons). Create a bulletin board with the portraits and their speech balloons under the caption: "The Best Thing About __________(fill in grade) Grade Is . . . ."

- Students can write about their favorite class memories on the wings of bumblebees. Display them with the caption: "_______(fill in grade) Grade Has Been Un-BEE-lievably Fun!" See pattern on page 26.

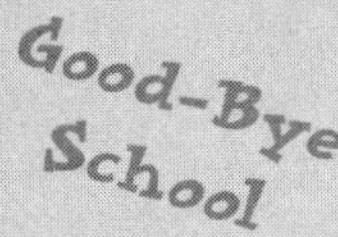

- Construct a semantic web with words your students think of when you say the word *good-bye*.

Historical Background

The actual last day of the school year varies from district to district or even state to state, but it is generally anywhere from the end of May to the middle of June.

Literary Exploration

Everett Anderson's Goodbye by Lucille Clifton
The Goodbye Book by Judith Viorst
Goodbye, Hello by Barbara Shook Hazen
Goodbye House by Frank Asch
Goodbye Max by Marit Kaldhol
Goodbye Mitch by Ruth Wallace-Brodeur
Goodbye Old Year, Hello New Year by Frank Modell
Goodbye Rune by Marit Kaldhol
The Goodbye Walk by Joanne Ryder
Hello, Goodbye by David Lloyd
Maggie and the Goodbye Gift by Sue Milord
And Peter Said Goodbye by Liz Farrington

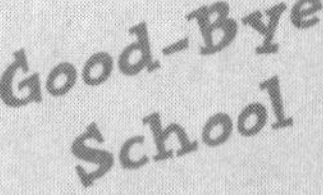

Writing Experience

- At the end of the year there are many things to do. Let students take part in the classroom "wrap-up," applying for the jobs they want to do. Post on a bulletin board the jobs that need to be done (gathering and counting math textbooks, cleaning the board, etc.). Let students write job resumes and applications to show why they should be picked for the jobs. You'll not only get students involved, you'll also increase writing skills.

- Let students write a letter to next year's class, telling about the kinds of things they can expect.

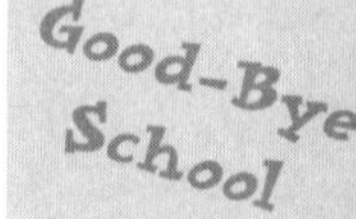

Writing Experience continued

• Let students compile an end-of-the-year memory book. Give them a cover to color and decorate. Each page can highlight a different area or subject.   (Examples: favorite book, favorite topic of study, favorite song, a happy memory) See patterns on pages 27-28.

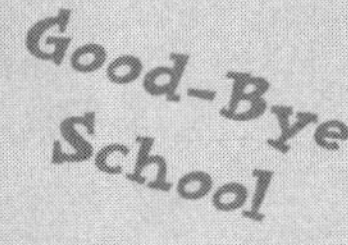

Math Experience

• Invite students to play a favorite math game they enjoyed during the year.

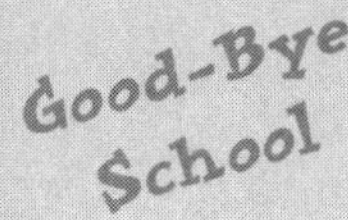

Social Studies Experience

• Work together to create a class time line, depicting the most memorable events of the year.

Music/Dramatic Experience

• Ask permission for your students to visit next year's teachers and class-rooms to alleviate anxiety. Arrange for them to interview students in that class to find out what the next grade will be like.

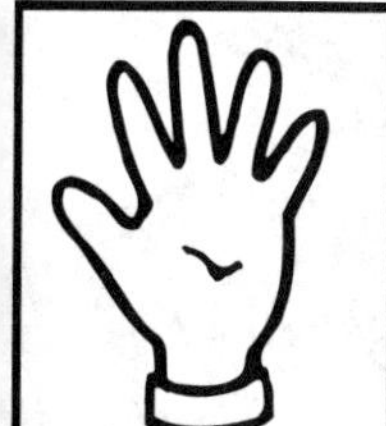

Physical/Sensory Experience

• Let students pick their favorite class games or sports to play today.

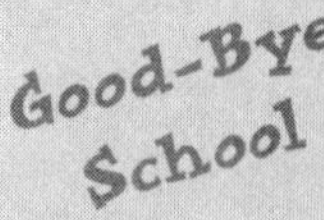

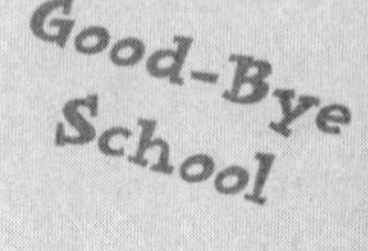

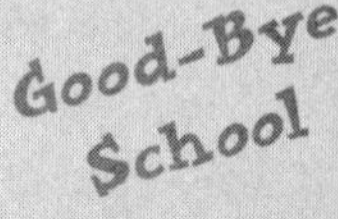

Arts/Crafts Experience

• Students can make their own graduation caps. They glue a square piece of cardboard covered in black material or paper to the top of a circular strip that has been fitted to each student's head. A yarn tassel can be added on top.

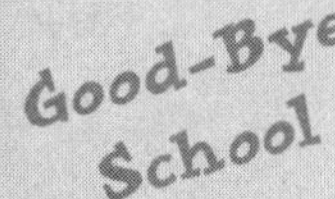
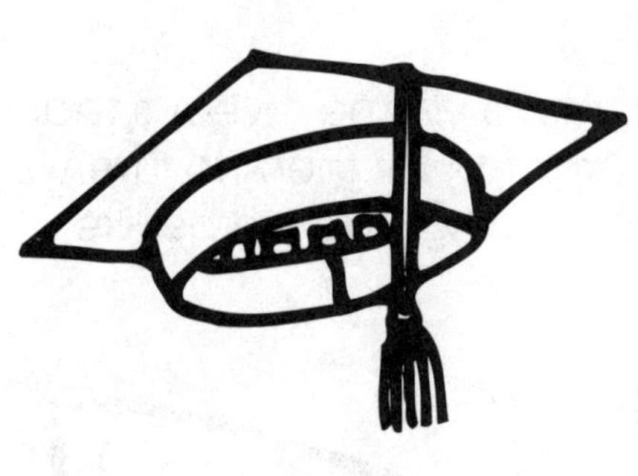
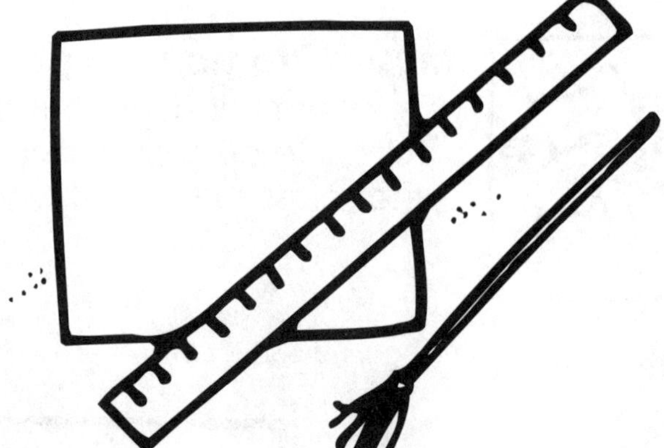

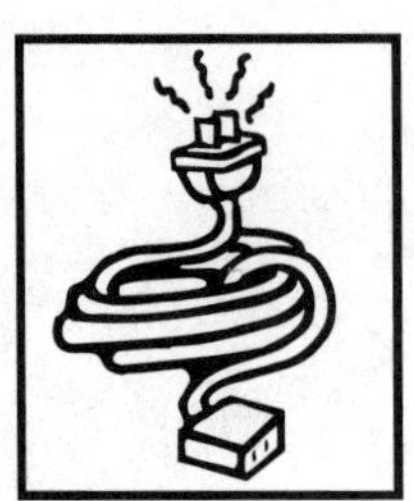

Extension Activities

• Hold your own graduation ceremony. Your students can make invitations for their families. Copy the graduation certificates on pages 29-30 to hand out at the ceremony. Borrow a sound recording of the music played at high school graduation ceremonies. Have students march in a processional. Choose a student to give a welcome, and have everyone sing the school song. Present the diplomas, then serve graduation cap cookies (see page 25). Let students sign their autographs in one another's class memory books. See patterns for certificate and invitation on pages 29-30.

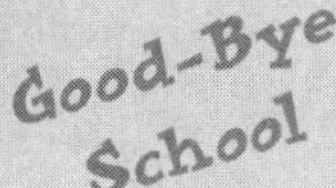

Extension Activities continued

⚠ Make yummy graduation cookies by using chocolate icing to attach a square of chocolate to a marshmallow, then attach the marshmallow to a chocolate-covered graham cracker. A licorice lace "tassel" can be added for a final "crowning" touch.

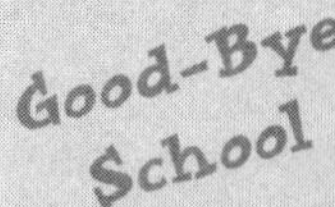

Values Education Experience

• Talk about the value of making new friends and appreciating old ones. Let volunteers share what they have learned from friends this year.

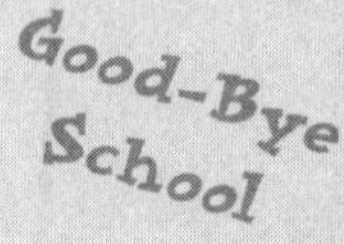

Follow-Up/Homework Idea

• Encourage your students to read like crazy all summer!

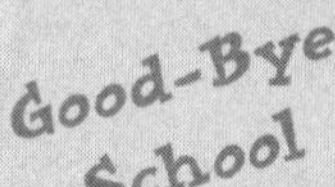

My most
un-bee-lievable
memory....
Name:

My
Book of
Memories

name:
Grade:
Teacher:
School Year:
Favorite Subjects:

Certificate of

Please come to my

Graduation!

For: _______________________________

Date: ________________ Time: ________

Place: _____________________________

Certificate of

Graduation!

Presented to:

____

For completing the _____ grade on the _____ day of ________________, 20 _____.

Teacher: _______________________

Principal: _______________________

Please come to my

Graduation!

For: _______________________

Date: ______________ Time: ______

Place: _______________________

Socrates' Birthday

June 5

Setting the Stage
- Construct a semantic web with facts your students know about Socrates.

Historical Background
The Greek philosopher, Socrates, was born on this day in 469 BC. Socrates was considered to be the wisest of the Greek philosophers. His student, another renowned Greek philosopher named Plato, recorded Socrates' writings so that we have them today. Socrates was known for his thirst for the beautiful and good. His ideas were somewhat radical for his day, and he was put to death because the rulers of Athens felt he was leading young people astray with his ideas. He was poisoned in 399 B.C.

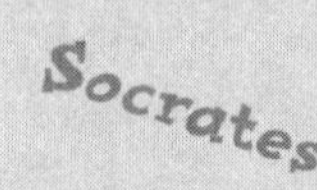

Literary Exploration

If I Were in Charge of the World and Other Worries: Poems for Children
    by Judith Viorst
Socrates by Rascal Bogaerts
Socrates by Robert Silverberg
Socrates and the Three Little Pigs by Tsuyoshi Mori

Language Experience

• How many new words can your students make using the letters in *Socrates*?

• Socrates looked for beautiful and good things. Have students brainstorm things that are beautiful and good. List them on the board, then have students alphabetize them.

Writing Experience

• Let students write their ideas of the meaning of life. See reproducible on page 35.

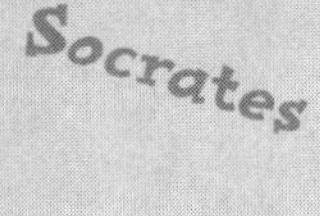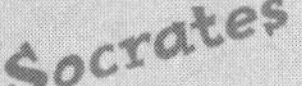

Math Experience

• Challenge students to figure out how old Socrates would be today. (He was born on this day in 469 B.C.)

• Have students use their subtraction skills to figure out how old Socrates was when he died. (He died in 399 B.C.)

Science/Health Experience

• Have students research poisons, including hemlock. Many household items are poisonous (such as drain cleaner, bleach, car coolant, etc.). Discuss the need to stay far away from poisonous things. How do we know they're poisonous? Bring some empty containers to show the warning labels.

Social Studies Experience

• Study some Greek philosophy.

• Create a time line showing where Socrates was in world history. Have students add other important dates and people.

• Have students locate Greece on a world map.

• Have students research Athens during the time of Socrates. What else was going on?

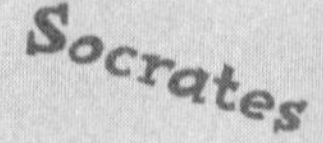

• Have students research other famous Greeks and share their findings with the rest of the class.

Music/Dramatic Experience

• Let students interview others about their philosophy of life.

• Let students work in pairs or small groups to write raps or songs to familiar tunes about the good/beautiful things in life.

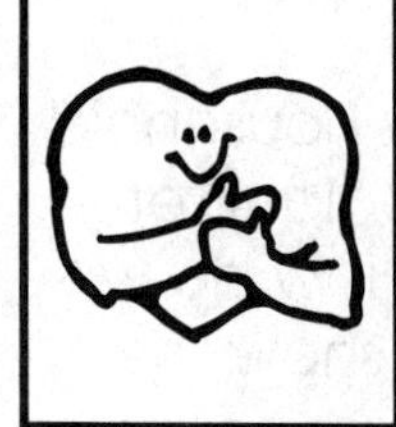

Values Education Experience

• Discuss what Socrates may have meant when he said, "know thyself." Why is that important?

Follow-Up/Homework Idea

• Encourage students to ask their parents about their philosophy of life.

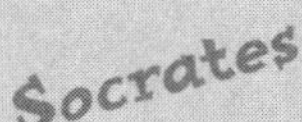

The
Meaning of life

World War II Day

June 6

Setting the Stage

- Display pictures and/or related literature about World War II.

- Construct a semantic web with words your students think of when you say the word *war*.

Historical Background

Today marks the date of the Allied D-Day Invasion in 1944 on the beaches of Normandy, France.

Literary Exploration

Americans in WWII 1944 by Edward Dolan
Behind the Secret Window: A Memoir of a Hidden Childhood During World War Two by Nelly S. Toll
But No Candy by Gloria Houston
The Children We Remember by Chana Byers
D-Day by Wallace Black
The First Book of World War II by Louis Snyder
Island on Bird Street by Uri Orlev
The Lily Cupboard by Shulamith Levey
Number the Stars by Lois Lowry
A Picture Book of Anne Frank by David A. Adler
Sadako and the Thousand Paper Cranes by Eleanor Coerr
Sheltering Rebecca by Mary Baylis-White
WW II by Louis Snyder
World War II Resistance Stories by Arthur Prager

Language Experience

- Throughout the war, much of the information between military groups had to be sent in code so the enemy would not know its message. Let your students make up their own codes (with numbers or letters) and write messages for others to figure out.

Writing Experience

- Ask students to write their feelings about war. See reproducible on page 40.

- Challenge students to write haiku poems about war. This unrhymed poetry form has just three lines. The first and third lines contain five syllables and the second line contains seven syllables. Example:
  War hurts everyone—
  Winners and losers alike.
  Let's all work for peace.

Math Experience

- Let students practice writing Roman numerals, as in World War II. How high can they go?

- Every year more of our World War II veterans die. Challenge students to figure out how old most veterans of that war are today. (There will be a range of ages depending on when they entered the war and their ages at the time.)

Science/Health Experience

- Have students research D-Day to discover what effect the weather had on the plans for it.

- What differences are there in the weapons and military tools of today with those available during World War II? Students can go online to research the topic and share their findings with the rest of the class.

Social Studies Experience

- Have students locate Normandy, France, on a world map.

- Study World War II, when it started, when the United States got into it and what countries were involved. Who were the Allied countries? Who were the Axis enemy countries?

Arts/Crafts Experience

• After reading, *Sadako and the Thousand Paper Cranes*, students can try making Japanese paper cranes. Look for instructions in a book about making origami.

• Let students work together to make a mural of a peaceful world.

Extension Activities

⚠ Students will enjoy "sundaes in helmets." Transform round paper bowls into World War II helmets for ice cream sundae bowls.

• Invite someone who remembers what World War II was like to share a firsthand account with your students.

Follow-Up/Homework Idea

• Encourage students to ask their grandparents or elderly relatives or neighbors about their memories of World War II.

WAR!

Merry Olde England Day

June 7

Setting the Stage

- Display a banner on your classroom door that says "Welcome to England!" Greet your students in royal fashion in a robe and crown. Call everyone (in an English accent, of course) "Duke" and "Duchess" or other royal names. Desks can be arranged in groups so students can be "royal families" for the day.

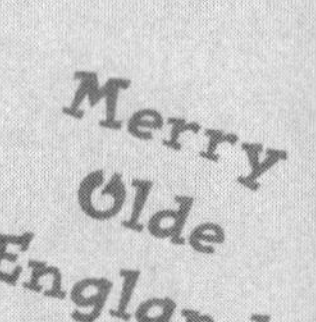

Setting the Stage continued

- Get travel brochures and posters about England from a local travel agency and display them around related literature.

- Construct a semantic web with facts your students know about England. Ask them to list questions they want answered today.

Historical Background

On this day in 1893, George Harbo and Frank Samuelson began a rowboat trip from New York City to England. They arrived nearly two months later. Though America and England fought in the American Revolution and again in the War of 1812, since that time the two countries have been friends and allies in other wars. From fish and chips to the queen to Harry Potter, Americans love all things British!

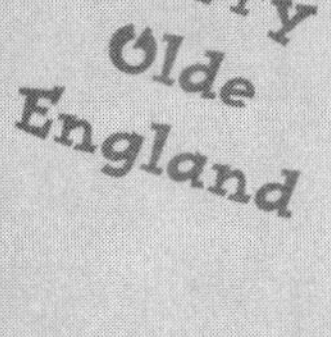

Literary Exploration

Anno's Britain by Mitsumasa Anno
Emily's Own Elephant by Phillippa Pearce
The Guard Mouse by Don Freeman
Land and People of England by Alicia Street
Let's Visit England by Garry Lyle
Long Meg by Rosemary Minard
Mary Poppins by P.L. Travers
Mary Poppins Comes Back by P.L. Travers
A Search for Two Bad Mice by Eleanor Clymer
The Story of an English Village by John S. Goodall
A Witch Got on at Paddington Station by Dyan Sheldon

Writing Experience
• Let students write what they think it would be like to be a king or queen. See reproducibles on pages 45-46.

Math Experience
• Have students practice counting "pence" (similar to an American penny) instead of pennies.

• Introduce other British money and have students compare it to American coins and currency.

Social Studies Experience
• Study the country of England and discover what makes it unique.

• Have students locate England on a world map and find out what countries are its closest neighbors.

Music/Dramatic Experience

• Sing the English nursery rhyme "Hot-Cross Buns."

> Hot-cross buns!
> Hot-cross buns!
> One a penny,
> Two a penny,
> Hot-cross buns!

Physical/Sensory Experience

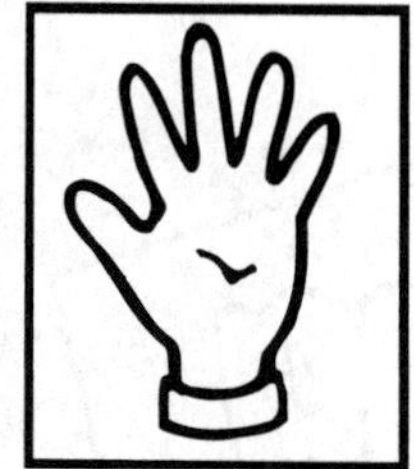

• Have students play one of England's favorite sports, soccer or rugby.

• Students can sing and play "London Bridge."

• Let students pretend to be British soldiers marching around the room and "changing the guard."

Arts/Crafts Experience

• Let each "royal family" group design a castle (exterior and interior) and family crest.

• Have students make British flags. Let volunteers find pictures of the flag on the internet.

Extension Activities

⚠ Serve English muffins with butter and cinnamon sugar or English trifle (layers of cake, pudding and whipped cream) for a tasty treat.

• Invite someone who has been to England to come and talk about it and share pictures and mementos with your class.

If I were King...

If I were Queen...

Ice Cream Day

June 8

Setting the Stage

- Display student work on a bulletin board with a giant ice cream cone and the caption:, "Here's the SCOOP on us!"

- Challenge students to read more books. Mount paper ice cream cones with student names on a wall. Every time a student reads a book and shares it with the class in an oral or written book report, then add an ice cream scoop to his cone. Students will enjoy making their ice cream cones go as high as possible! See patterns on pages 55-56.

- On a permanent bulletin board, display ice cream cones with suggestions on proofreading writing papers before turning them in. Each cone can have a different reminder on it. (Examples: Begin each sentence with a capital letter. Check your spacing. Make sure each sentence is a complete thought. Check for needed punctuation.)

- Construct a semantic web with facts your students know (or would like to know) about ice cream.

Historical Background

The first commercially made ice cream was advertised for the first time in the United States in New York City on this day in 1786, though the first ice cream come didn't come along for another 120 years or so.

Literary Exploration

Curious George Goes to an Ice Cream Shop by Margret Rey
Ice Cream by William Jaspersohn
Ice Cream by Stella Keller
Ice Cream Cows and Mitten Sheep by Jane Belk Moncure
Ice Cream Is Falling by Shigeo Watanabe
The Ice Cream Ocean by Susan Russo
Ice Cream Soup by Gail Herman
Ice Cream Soup by Frank Modell
The Ice Cream Store by Dennis Lee
I Love Ice Cream by C.V. Hall
Land Where the Ice Cream Grows by Anthony Burgess
Scoop After Scoop: A History of Ice Cream by Stephen Krensky
The Scoop on Ice Cream by Vicki Cobb
Striped Ice Cream by Lexau
Too Hot for Ice Cream by Jean Van Leeuwen

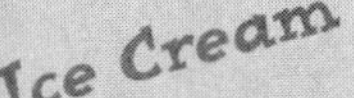

48

Language Experience

• Let students brainstorm their favorite ice cream flavors. List them on the board, then have students put them in alphabetical order.

Writing Experience

• Have students write about "The Most Unusual Ice Cream Sundae." See reproducible on page 57.

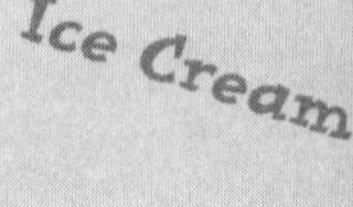

Math Experience

• Students can take a poll to see what students around the school prefer, ice cream in a bowl or a cone. Have them add their findings to a class bar graph.

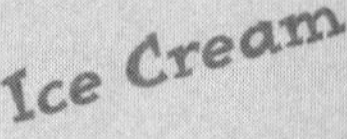

Math Experience continued

• Hand out ice cream and cones from pages 55-56. Students write math sums on the cones, then put math problems equivalent to the sums on ice cream scoops. (Example: 16 on a cone and scoops with 10 + 6, 8 + 8, 4 x 4 on them) Students can put all their ice cream scoops in a common pile and mix them up, then try to make their matches.

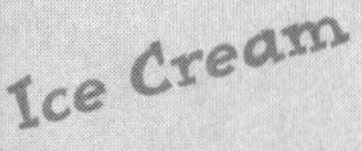

Social Studies Experience

• Study the history of ice cream. Your students may not be aware that ice cream or a variation of it has been around since 64 A.D., when Nero was emperor of Rome. Nero sent slave armies to get snow and ice from the mountains to cool his fruit drinks. Legend has it that by accident, one of the drinks froze overnight and the icy treat was born! Later in the 13th century, Marco Polo apparently returned from China with ice cream recipes. They were a favorite among rich Europeans and came to the New World with the English colonists. Most people could not afford to make their own ice cream until Nancy Johnson came along. She made ice cream more accessible by inventing a freezer for it in 1848. Three years later, Jacob Fussell, established the first ice cream factory. The cone was introduced at the World's Fair in St. Louis, Missouri, in 1904. Since then, ice cream has been a part of American tradition and culture. More ice cream is eaten in the United States than any other country in the world.

Music/Dramatic Experience

• Students can create advertisements for new ice cream flavors of the month and try to convince other students to buy them.

Physical/Sensory Experience

⚠ Try making homemade ice cream. Students place 1 cup of milk, 1 cup of whipped cream, $1/2$ teaspoon of vanilla and $1/2$ cup of sugar with any fruit or flavored syrup in a 1-pound metal can with a tightly sealed lid. They place the can inside a 3-pound metal can, then pack crushed ice around the smaller can. They pour a cup of rock salt over the crushed ice, then put the lid on the larger can. Students roll the can back and forth for about 15 minutes. (The mixture can be stirred intermittently throughout the process.) When the mixture is frozen enough, it will be ready to eat.

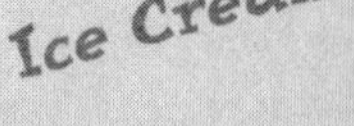

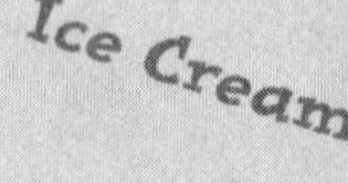

Arts/Crafts Experience

• Let students draw, paint or use clay to make illustrations of their dream ice cream sundaes!

Extension Activities

⚠ If you make homemade ice cream, you might want to try one of the following recipes:

Country Vanilla Ice Cream

2 1/4 c. sugar	1 pint cream
4 eggs	4 1/2 t. salt
7 c. milk	

Beat eggs and sugar gradually until stiff. Add remaining ingredients. Mix and pour into freezer. Makes 5 quarts.

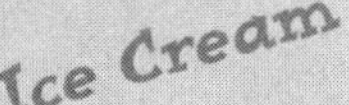

Tutti Fruiti Ice Cream

1 small pkg. strawberry Jell-O™

1 small can crushed pineapple, drained

2 diced bananas

1 small can lemonade concentrate

1 can evaporated milk

1 pint whipping cream

Mix and freeze!

1 c. water

2 c. sugar

1 c. nuts

Fresh Peach Ice Cream

2 1/2 c. pureed peaches

2 c. sugar

1/2 c. lemon juice

1/2 c. orange juice

Combine ingredients above and chill.

Then combine 1 pint whipping cream and freeze.

Rocky Road Ice Cream

3 c. whipping cream

3/4 c. chocolate syrup

1/2 c. sweetened condensed milk

1 t. vanilla

1 1/2 c. miniature marshmallows

1/2 c. chopped walnuts

3 oz. mini chocolate chips

Mix and spoon into freezer.

Peach and Banana Freeze

1¹/4 c. fresh peaches

1 c. mashed bananas

3 oz. can of lemonade concentrate

¹/4 c. sugar

¹/4 t. banana flavoring

1 c. whipping cream

Mix and pour into freezer.

Follow-Up/Homework Idea

- Students can suggest to their parents that they go out for ice cream for dessert tonight.

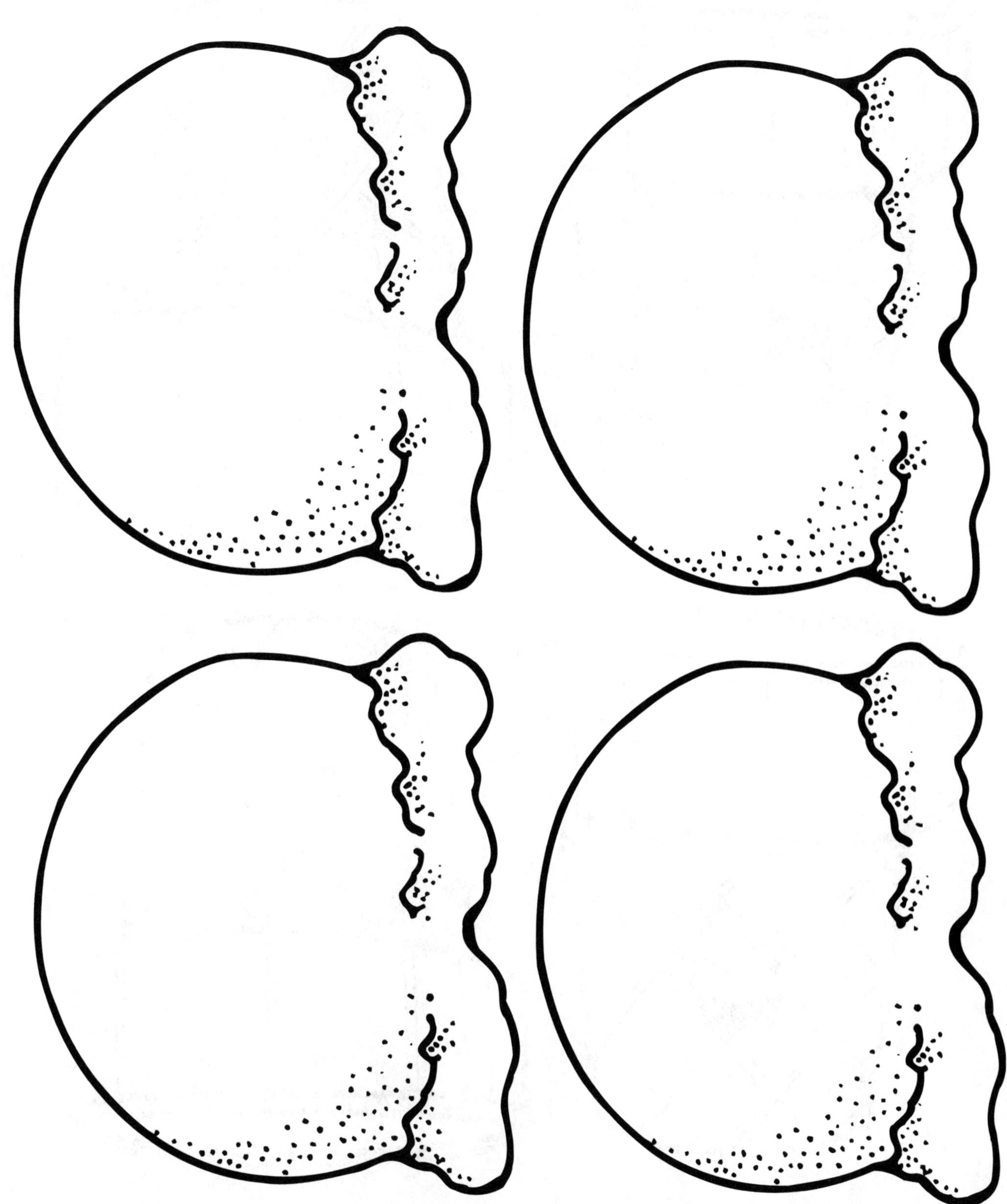

The Most Unusual Ice Cream Sundae

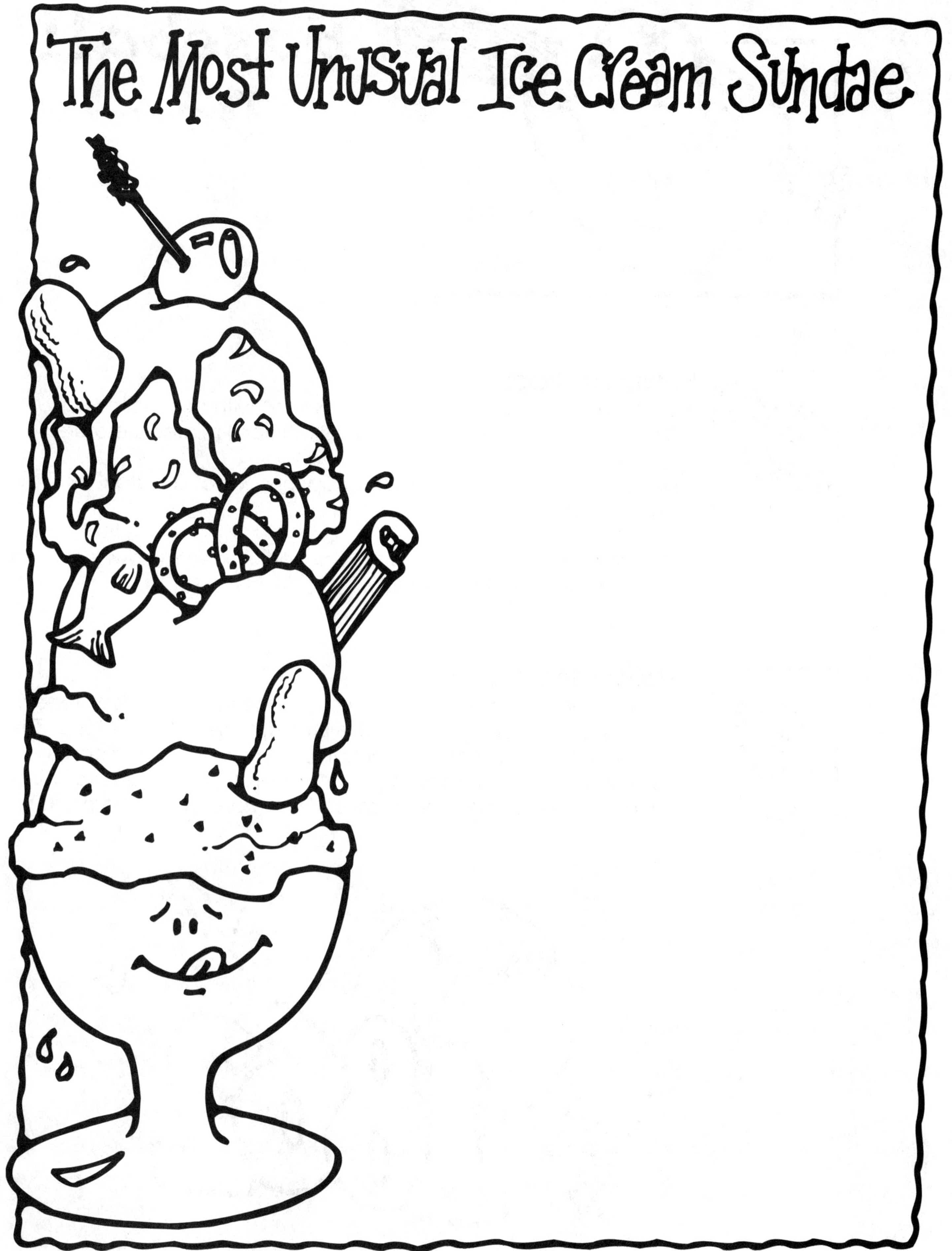

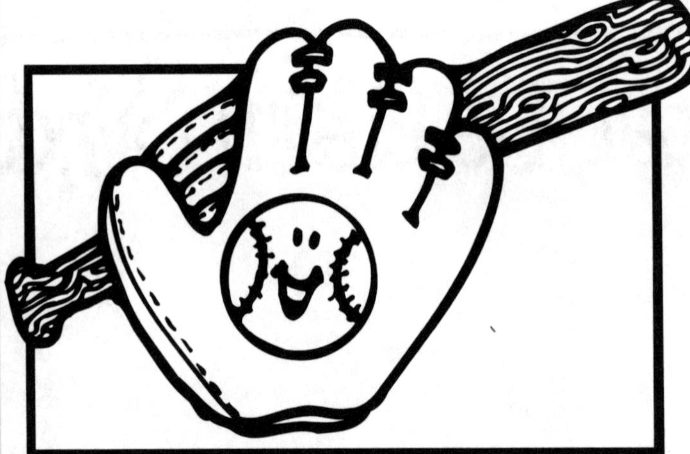

Baseball Day

June 9

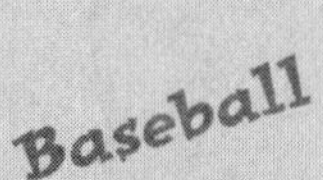

Setting the Stage

- Celebrate the "Great American pastime" with baseball today. Display baseball equipment around baseball-related literature.

- Display student work around the caption: "What a Catch" or "What a Hit!"

- Construct a semantic web with facts your students know (or would like to know) about baseball.

Historical Background

The first recorded baseball game was played in 1846 in New Jersey. The first baseball stadium opened in Brooklyn, New York, in 1862. The team became known as the Brooklyn Dodgers. Today baseball is known as the nation's pastime. Over 50 million people attend major league baseball games and many millions more watch them on TV.

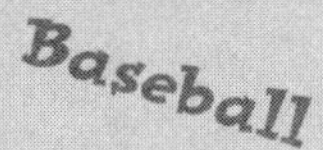

Literary Exploration

All About Baseball by George Sullivan
Baseball Brothers by Jeff Rubin
Baseball Saved Us by Ken Mochizuki
Baseball Tips by Dean Hughes
Baseball: You Are the Manager by Nate Aaseng
Curious George Plays Baseball by Margret Rey
The Field Beyond the Outfield by Mark Teague
Frank and Ernest Play Ball by Alexandra Day
The Story of Baseball by Lawrence Ritter
Teammates by Peter Golenbock
The Year of the Boar by Betty Bao Lord

Language Experience

• A baseball bat and ball shapes can be used to help reinforce writing skills you are currently working on (contractions, plurals, etc.). For example, one student can write a compound word on a baseball and another writes the two words that make up its equivalent on a baseball bat. Students can add these to a common pile and mix them up before making matches again.

• Let your students brainstorm as many words as they can that rhyme with *bat*.

Writing Experience

• Encourage students to imagine explaining how baseball is played to a person who has never heard of the game. They can write the baseball rules in clear, concise words. See reproducible on page 63.

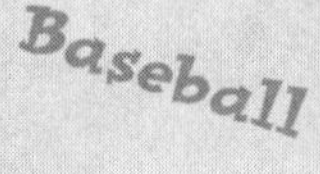

Math Experience

- Play Math Baseball. Divide students into two teams. Challenge them to get on bases by answering math facts. If students want to try for a "home run," they'll get an advanced math problem. See patterns on page 64.

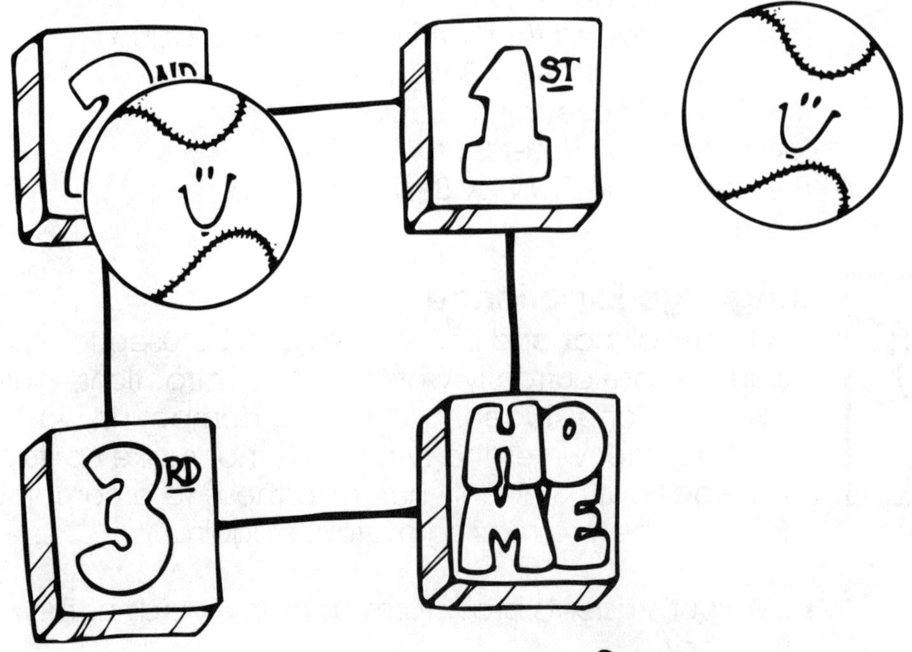

- Older students can work together to measure the area and perimeter of a baseball field.

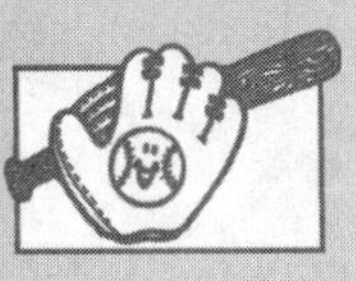

Science/Health Experience

- Review baseball safety.

- Discuss how playing baseball is good exercise—running, stretching, throwing the ball, etc.

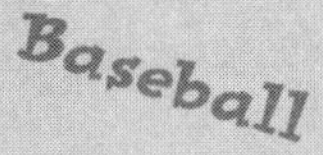

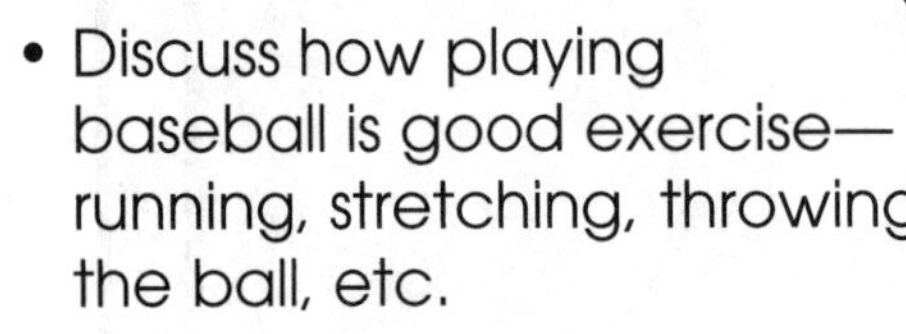
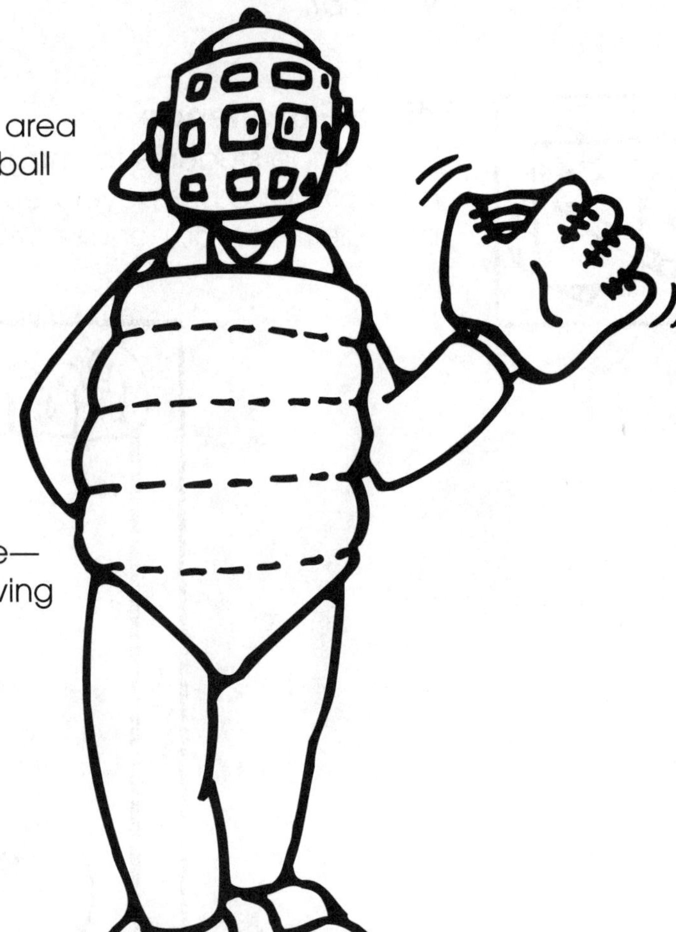

Social Studies Experience
• Study the history of baseball. Your students will be interested to know that the first baseball team uniforms consisted of straw hats, white shirts and blue trousers.

Music/Dramatic Experience
• Sing the song "Take Me Out to the Ball Game."

Physical/Sensory Experience
• Let students practice pitching a ball with elaborate windups and follow-throughs.

• If weather permits, challenge another class to a game of outdoor baseball.

Arts/Crafts Experience
• Let students draw a class mural of a baseball game in their favorite baseball park.

Extension Activities

⚠ No baseball day would be complete without baseball goodies! Serve bagged popcorn, Cracker Jacks™, pretzels, peanuts in the shell, soda pop and hot dogs.

• Invite a high school baseball player or coach to visit your class and talk about the game of baseball.

⚠ In honor of baseball great Babe Ruth, serve miniature Baby Ruth™ candy bars.

• Invite students to wear their favorite baseball team caps and T-shirts today.

Values Education Experience

• Baseball players, other athletes and entertainers make much more money than most Americans. How do your students feel about this? What does this indicate about our value system? Do they deserve more money than fire fighters, police officers and other hard-working people?

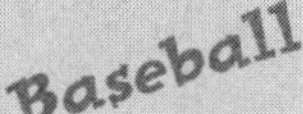

Follow-Up/Homework Idea

• Encourage students to play baseball with their friends or family members after school.

Game Rules

1ST
2ND
3RD
HO ME

Making Sense Day

June 10

Setting the Stage
- Display items that students must use one or more of their senses to investigate. (Examples: feather—touch, bell—hearing, popcorn—taste)

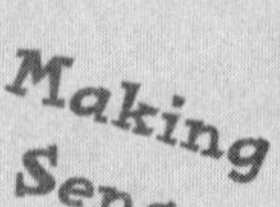

Literary Exploration
The City Noisy Book by Margaret Wise Brown
Crunch, Crunch by Ethel Kessler
First Delight: A Book About the Five Senses by Tasha Tudor
I Hear by Louise and Thoburn Ogle
If You Listen by Charlotte Zolotow
Indoor Noisy Book by Margaret Wise Brown
My Five Senses by Aliki
My Five Senses by Margret Miller
Sounds All Around by Jane Belk Moncure
A Tasting Party by Jane Belk Moncure
The Touch Book by Jane Belk Moncure
What Your Nose Knows by Jane Belk Moncure
Your Amazing Senses by Ron Van derMeer

Language Experience

- Let one student blindfold another. The person who can see must explain how to do a specific project through verbal directions only. The blindfolded person tries to follow the directions.

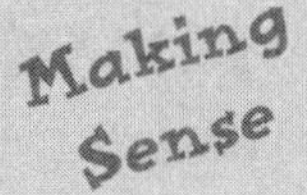

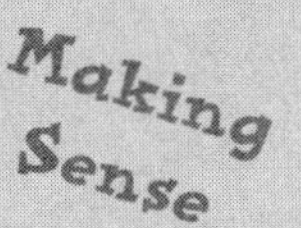

Writing Experience

- Students can write about what they think it would be like to be without one or more of their senses. Students can be blindfolded, stuff cotton in their ears, plug their noses or even have their hands tied behind their backs to help them see how much they use their senses. See reproducible on page 69.

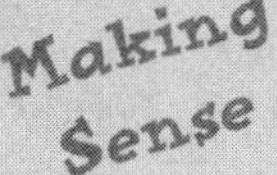

Social Studies Experience

• Let students research famous people throughout history who were limited in one of their senses (sight, hearing, etc.). Have them share with the class how the person coped with his or her limitations.

Music/Dramatic Experience

• Play a musical recording of various sounds to see if students can identify them.

Physical/Sensory Experience

• Create a "feely" bag or box with items of various textures. Students can try to distinguish each item based on touch only.

• Have students close their eyes, then listen carefully to sounds to help them identify items. (Examples: scrunching up paper or opening a soda can)

• Play I Spy and let students use their eyes to scan the room to identify the secret object you describe in the room.

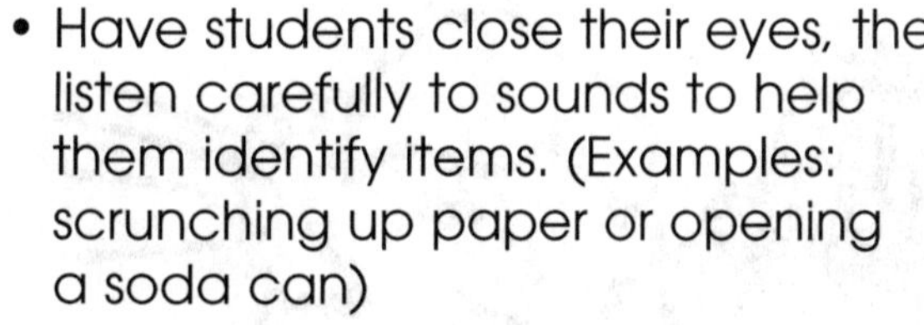

Arts/Crafts Experience

• Students can draw self-portraits, labeling areas of the body and explaining how their senses help them.

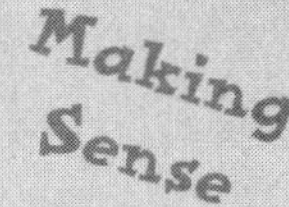

Extension Activities

• Go on a nature walk with your class to discover firsthand how much you use your senses.

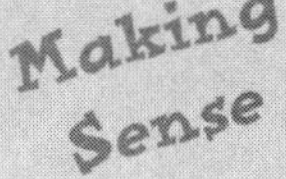

TASTE · Smell · Touch
SOUND
Sight
SOUND
Sight
TASTE · Smell · Touch

Jacques Cousteau's Birthday

June 11

Setting the Stage

- Display student work on an ocean background with a giant whale and the caption: "A Whale of a Job!" or "Work Worth SPOUTING Over" or "SEA How Much We Are Learning!"

- Create a permanent bulletin board showing an octopus with outstretched arms labeled with classroom duties and the caption: "Lend a Helping Hand!"

- Students are fascinated with ocean creatures, so capitalize on this natural interest with a display of literature books, posters and ocean paraphernalia (snorkels, diving equipment).

Setting the Stage continued
- Drape blue cellophane from the ceiling and let students use fishing line to suspend handmade ocean creatures along with seaweed for an interesting and colorful display. Or just hang the sea creatures all over your ceiling for an "in the aquarium" feel. See fish patterns on pages 79-84.

- Construct a semantic map or web of information your students know about the ocean. Ask them to list questions they would like answered to help you structure the day's activities.

Historical Background
Jacques-Yves Cousteau was a French oceanographer born on this day in 1910. His television programs about ocean life introduced the world to a part of the Earth they had never seen before.

Literary Exploration

Animals of the Sea by Mareelle Verite
The Blue Whale by Donna Grosvenor
Call It Courage by Armstrong Sperry
Catch a Baby Whale by the Tail by Edward R. Ricciuti
The Cay by Theodore Taylor
Dale the Whale by Bob Reese
Dancing with Manatees by Faith McNulty
Fish Is Fish by Leo Lionni
The Friendly Dolphins by Patricia Lauber
How To Hide an Octopus and Other Sea Creatures by Ruth Heller
I Am the Ocean by Suzanna Marshak
Ibis: A True Whale Story by John Himmelman
In the Ocean by Claire Henley
Inside the Whale and Other Animals by Ted Dewan
Island of the Blue Dolphins by Scott O'Dell
Jacques Cousteau by Genie Iverson
Jacques Cousteau: Champion of the Sea by Catherine Reef
Jacques Cousteau, Man of the Oceans by Carol Greene
Look Inside the Ocean by Laura Crema
Magic School Bus on the Ocean Floor by Joanna Cole
A Million Fish . . . More or Less by Patricia C. McKissack
The Ocean Alphabet Book by Jerry Palotta
Ocean Animals by Michael Chinery
Ocean Day by Shelly Rotner and Ken Kreisler
Ocean Life by David Cook
Ocean Parade: A Counting Book by Patricia MacCarthy
An Ocean World by Peter Sis
Physty: The True Story of a Young Whale's Rescue by Richard Ellis
The Rainbow Fish by Marcus Pfister
Rivers and Oceans by Barbara Taylor
Sam the Sea Cow by Francine Jacobs
A Sea Full of Sharks by Betsy Maestro
See the Ocean by Estelle Condra
Sukey and the Mermaid by Robert San Souci
Swimmy by Leo Lionni
Treasures of the Sea by National Geographic
Uncle Louie's Fantastic Sea Voyage by Jan Loof
The Whale in the Ocean by Jasper Tomkins
Whale Is Stuck by Karen Hayles
Whales in Danger by J.M. Roever
The Whale's Song by Dyan Sheldon
The Whale Tale by John Stevenson
What's Inside? Sea Creatures by Dorling Kindersley
The Wild Baby Goes to Sea by Barbro Lindgren

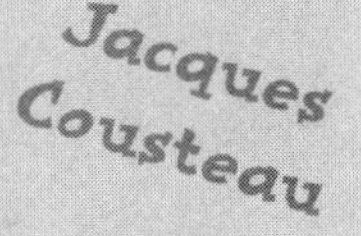

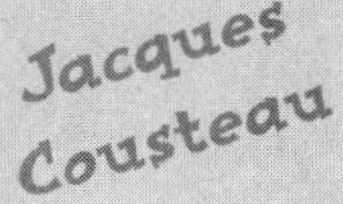

Language Experience

- Create a class Venn diagram depicting the similarities and differences between a shark and a whale.

- Challenge your students to list and alphabetize the seven major oceans.

Writing Experience

- Students can write about their own deep sea-diving adventure and tell what they might see "deep in the sea." See reproducible on page 85.

Math Experience

- Let students measure out the area and perimeter of a whale with bright yarn on the school play area. Then they can stand inside to see the actual size of this ocean beast. A small group can act out the part of the fins, while other groups simulate the action of the tail, the spout and the mouth for a little added fun!

Science/Health Experience

• Begin a study of the animal life found in the ocean.

• Study plant life found in the ocean.

• Learn about characteristics of the ocean (depths, mineral content and temperatures) and the ocean floor.

• Illustrate how the principle of buoyancy in seawater works. Drop a raw egg in a glass of fresh water and in a glass filled with water that contains $1/3$ cup of salt. The egg in salt water will float rather than sink.

• Use a sieve to demonstrate how a whale's baleen works.

Social Studies Experience

• Let students research man's dependence (throughout history) on the ocean for survival.

• Have students locate the main bodies of water (seven oceans) on a world map. How do these bodies of water differ?

• Share a short biographical sketch about Jacques Cousteau or check out one of his videos from a library to watch.

Music/Dramatic Experience

• Secure a recording of whale sounds with *Songs of the Humpback Whale* or *Deep Voices* by Capitol Records.

Physical/Sensory Experience

• For a "wave-like" sensation, have students fill clean, clear two-liter soda bottles about halfway with water and blue food coloring. They can add a few drops of baby oil to the mixture, then secure the top tightly. If they start a slight rocking motion to the bottle, it will resemble the gentle motion of an ocean wave.

• If you play whale songs for your students, they can ripple blue crepe paper for a wave-like rhythm to the music.

• Play a game of Tentacles. Put half of the class on one side of the playing field and the rest on the other side. Choose an "Octopus" to stand in the middle laying in wait to catch anyone trying to cross to the shore on the other side. Those who are caught become the "Octopuses" tentacles, catching others. The game is complete when only one person is still free.

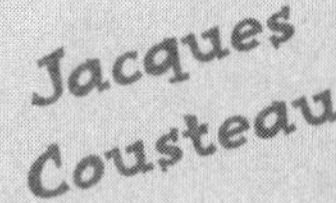

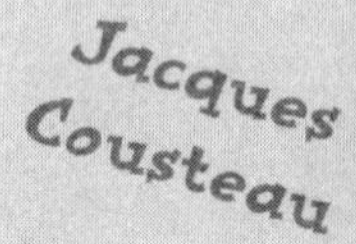

Arts/Crafts Experience

• Create underwater pictures. Students cut ocean animals, fish and plants from construction paper and place them between two pieces of waxed paper. They add green and blue crayon shavings to surround the ocean creatures. An adult irons them with a warm iron to seal the shapes and crayon shavings in place. Placed in front of a window for beautiful window displays.

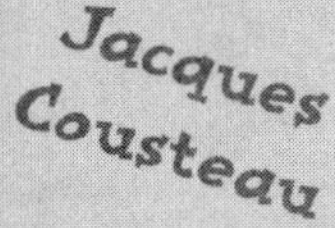

• Students can create pictures by wetting white construction paper, then painting, allowing colors to "bleed" together. While the paper is still wet, salt grains can be tossed onto the paper. When the paper is dry, students cut out paper fish shapes and add them. Then they mount the pictures on dark construction paper backgrounds.

• Have students paint ocean murals depicting the three basic regions: surface water or "sunlight" zone, the middle section or "twilight zone" and the depths or "midnight zone." Let them paint the ocean animals and plants that are able to live in each section.

• Let students draw whales or sharks and identify the body parts and their functions. Students can make "flip-top" creatures by tracing duplicate patterns and stapling them at the top over the picture. The external view of the whale or shark can be "lifted" to reveal its insides.

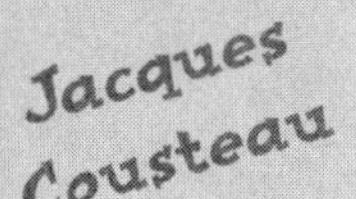

Arts/Crafts Experience continued

- Create a class submarine from a large appliance box. Cut out large, round portholes to view the surrounding ocean. Cover them with plastic wrap. Suspend ocean animals and fish from the ceiling or over the portholes to simulate underwater marine life. Cover the inside of the sub with dark butcher paper and draw "dials and fixtures" for an authentic feel. Put books or ocean materials inside with a flashlight as an incentive for students to read.

- Students can create dioramas of underwater scenes in shoe boxes.

- To make colorful jellyfish, students can shear thin colored ribbon (to make it curly), then glue the ribbon to the rim of a painted paper plate.

Arts/Crafts Experience continued

• Make ocean scenes in jars! Students put modeling clay on the lids of baby food jars, stick plastic ocean creatures and plants in it and fill it with water. The lids are then screwed on tightly and the jars are turned upright. Presto! Ocean in a jar!

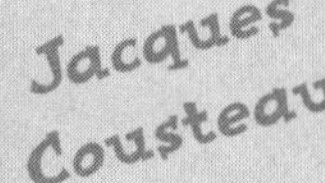

Extension Activities

• Most grocery stores sell goldfish crackers and SharkleBerry Fin Kool-Aid™ to share with your students as a light snack.

• Gel-set "gummy fish" in clear plastic cups of blue Jell-O™ for an edible ocean.

• Invite an oceanographer to visit your class to talk about his or her work.

• If there is an aquarium or marine life exhibit nearby, take your class there for a field trip.

Follow-Up/Homework Idea

• Encourage students to check out books about ocean life to take home.

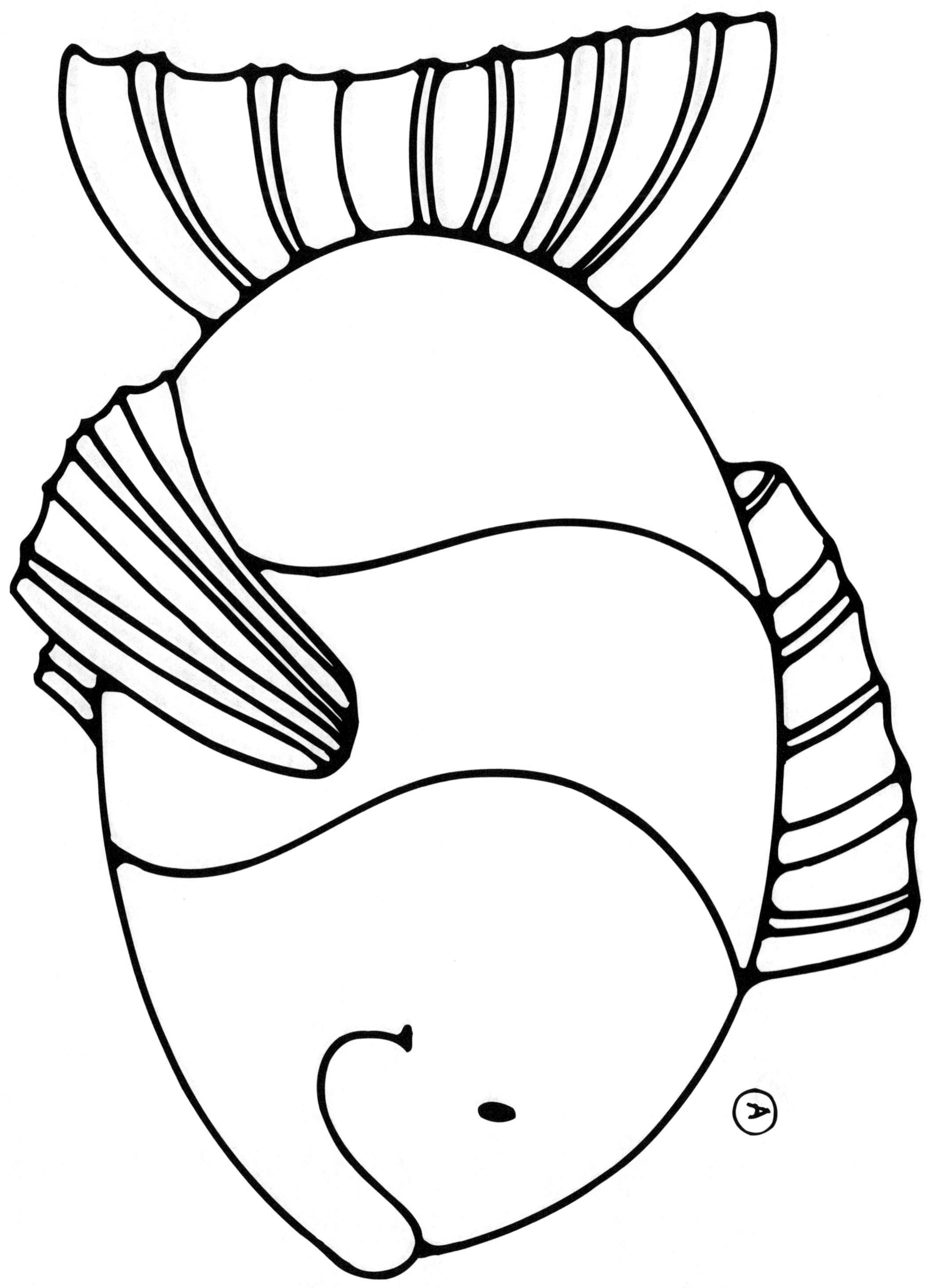

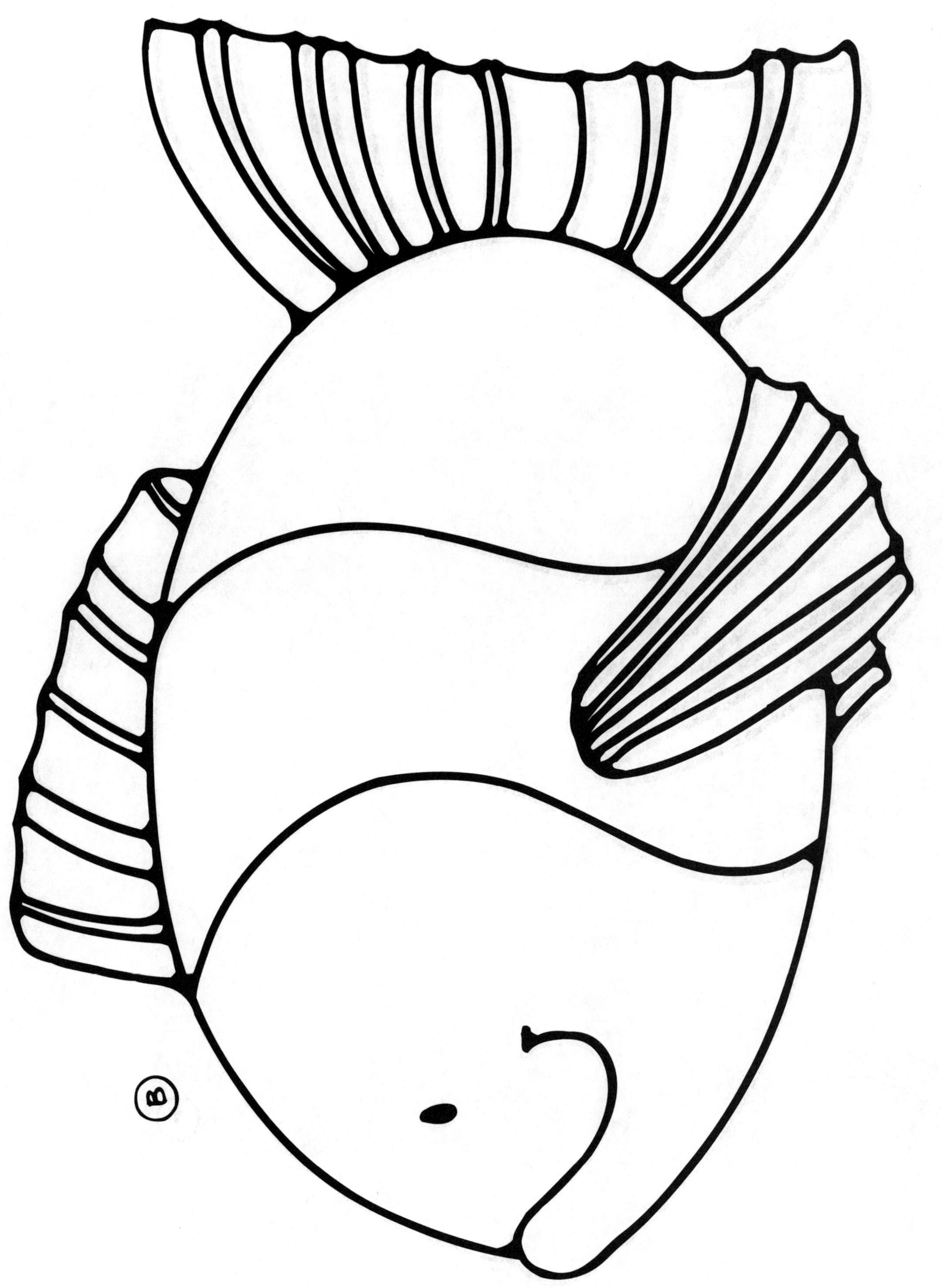

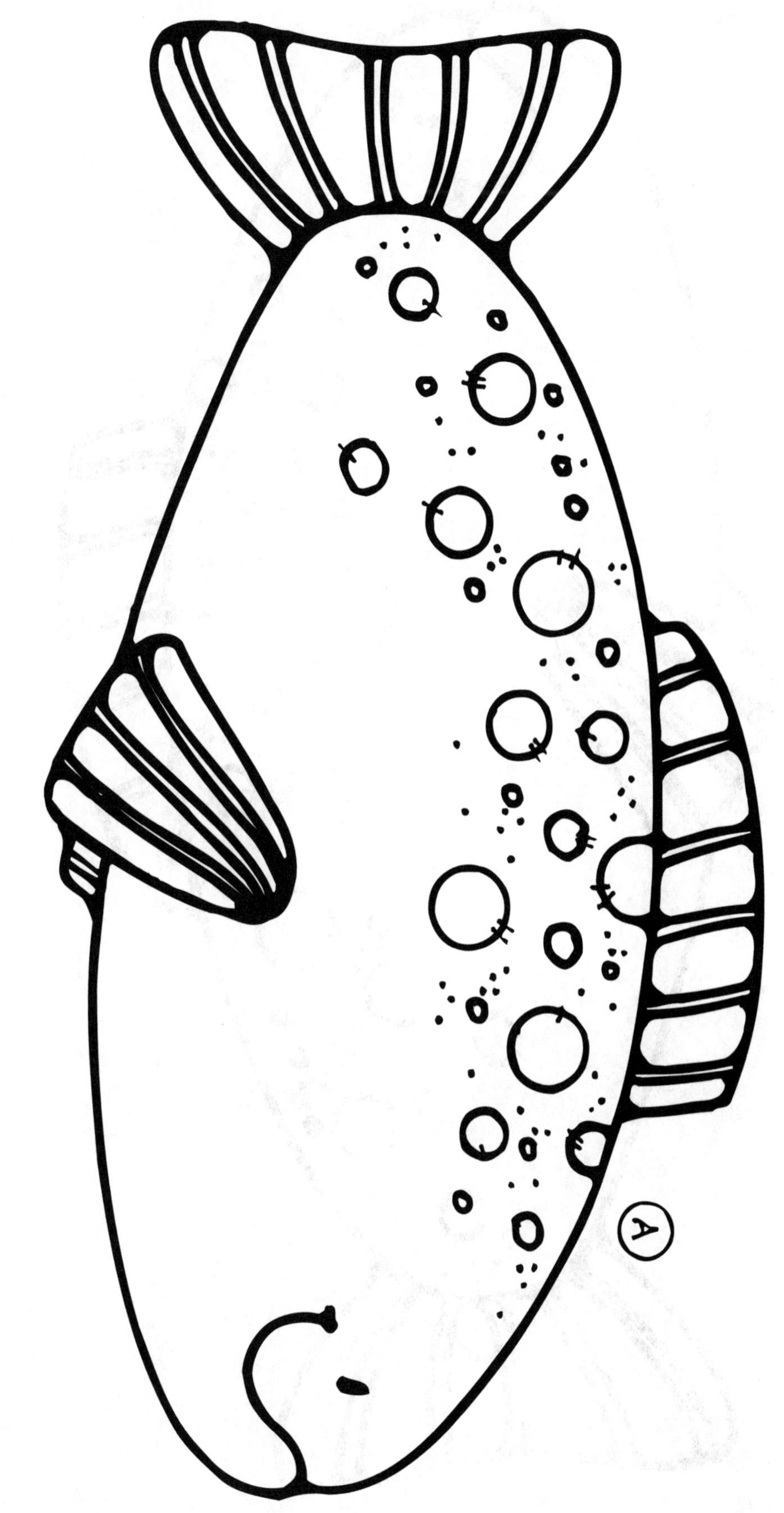
A

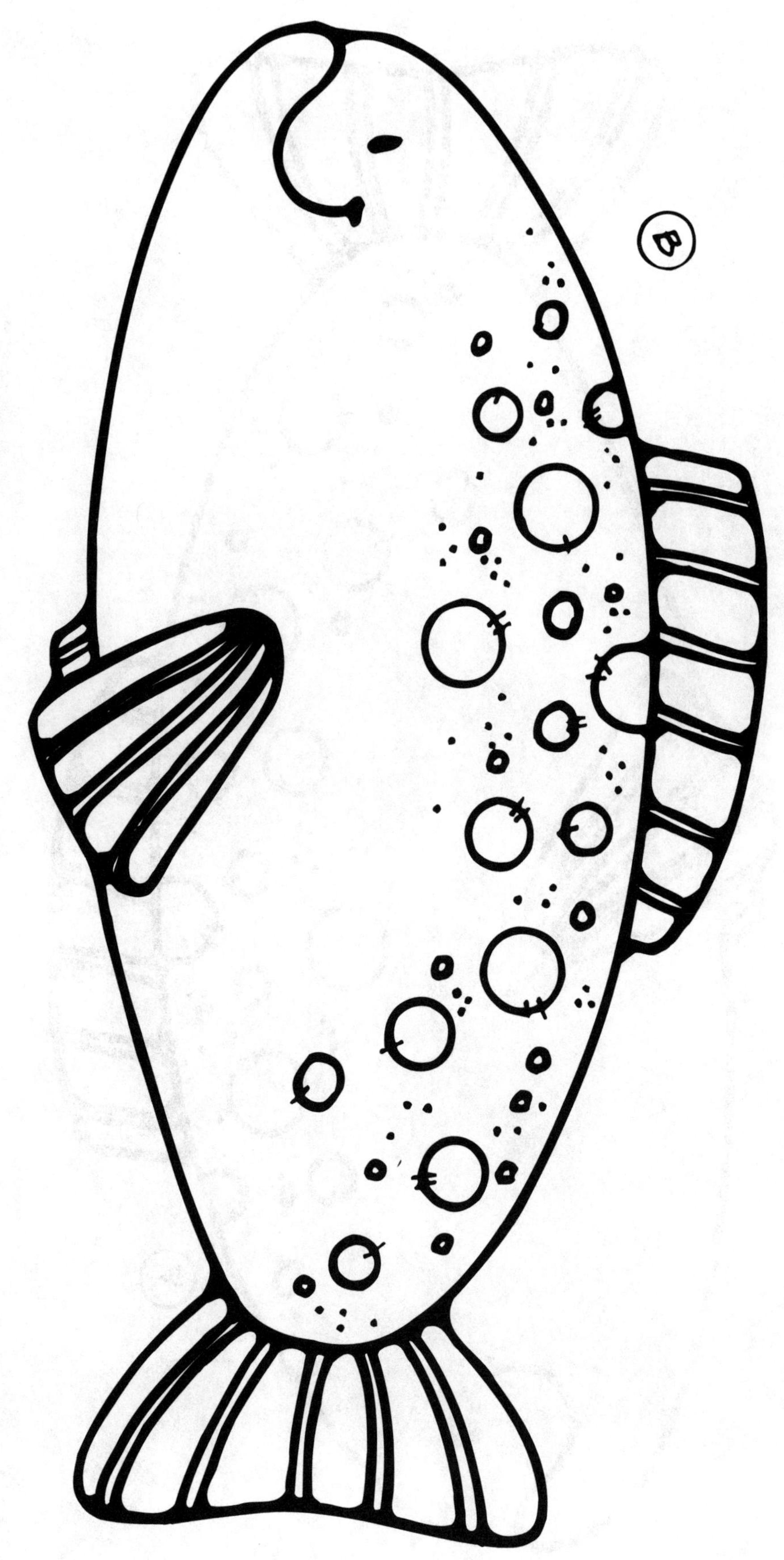

82

A

Deep in the Sea

Movin' on Day

June 12

Setting the Stage

- Display pictures of people moving surrounded by related literature to gather excitement about today's emphasis.

- Construct a semantic web with facts your students know (or would like to know) about moving.

Historical Background

Some people live their whole lives in the same house. Many others move several times during their life to different cities, states and even countries. America is a nation of people on the move. In 2003 14 percent of U.S. residents moved. However that is the lowest rate since the Census Bureau began collecting the data in 1948. In 1948 about 21 percent of Americans moved.

Literary Exploration

The Berenstain Bears' Moving Day by Stan Berenstain
Everett Anderson's Goodbye by Lucille Clifton
Family Moving Day by Genevieve Huriet
Goodbye, Hello by Barbara Shook Hazen
Goodbye, House by Frank Asch
Hello, Goodbye by David Lloyd
I'm Moving by Martha Whitmore Hickman
I'm Not Moving, Mama! by Nancy White Carstrom
Ira Says Goodbye by Bernard Waber
Maggie Doesn't Want to Move by Elizabeth O'Donnell
Melanie Mouse's Moving Day by Cyndy Szekeres
Mitchell Is Moving by Marjorie Weinman Sharmat
Moving by Fred Rogers
Moving by Michael Rosen
Moving by Wendy Watson
Moving Day by Tobi Tobias
Moving House by Kate Petty
Moving to Town! by Mattie Lou O'Kelley
My Best Friend Moved Away by Joy Zelonky
A New Home, A New Friend by Hans Wilhelm
And Peter Said Goodbye by Liz Farrington
Teddy Bear's Moving Day by Susanna Gretz
Things to Know Before You Move by Lisa Marsoli

Language Experience

• Create a Venn diagram depicting the similarities and differences between moving in and moving out of a house.

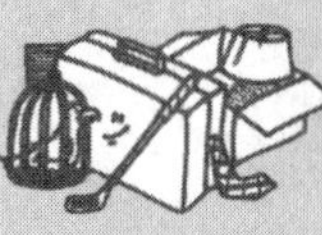

Writing Experience

- Let students brainstorm, then categorize items that would have to be moved from an old house to a new house (pets, furniture, dishes, toys and games, clothes, etc.).

- Let students speculate on what they would take if they had to move at a moment's notice because of a pending disaster. All they can take is what they can carry. What is so important, they couldn't do without it? See reproducible on page 92.

Math Experience

- Let students have a "moving" experience in math today. Let them estimate distances between areas in the room and then measure to see how close their estimations were. Then let them move their desks to new places in the room.

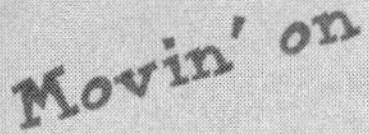

Science/Health Experience

- Discuss feelings students might have if they had to move away from their present homes (old memories, loneliness for old friends, new anxieties).

- Review moving safety (carrying heavy objects, sharp corners).

Social Studies Experience

• Let students review mapping skills by mapping out their old bedrooms, then projecting on a map what their new bedrooms would be like.

• Gather maps and travel brochures and put them in a classroom center. Students can look at them and think about places around the world that would be fun to move to.

Music/Dramatic Experience

• Create a "Welcome Wagon" for new students who move into your classroom. Fill an old wagon with student supplies (crayons, class rules or suggestions, map of school, books, pencils, a class picture, etc.). Students can make cards or pictures to welcome the new student to your classroom.

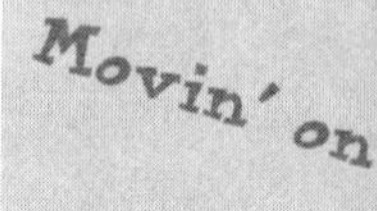

Physical/Sensory Experience

- Have a "moving" relay race. Divide students into teams and give each team a suitcase full of large-sized clothes and accessories. Players race to open the suitcase, put on the clothes, then "travel" to the new home (designated area). Then they take off the travel clothes, put them back in the suitcase and "travel" to the next people on their teams.

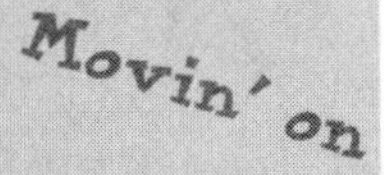

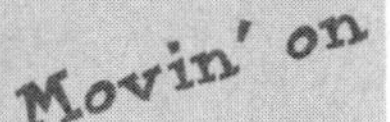

Arts/Crafts Experience

- Students will enjoy drawing pictures of their homes and neighborhoods. They can keep the pictures in their scrapbooks for future memories if they ever move away.

- Students can make collages from magazine pictures or drawings of things they would want to be sure to pack if they moved to new homes.

Extension Activities

- Invite a representative from a moving company to visit your class to tell about his or her work.

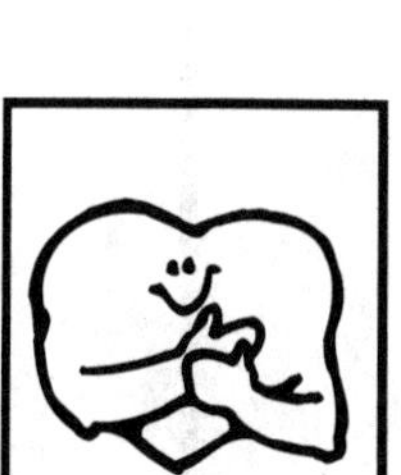

Values Education Experience

- This is a good time to talk about valuing our families, no matter where we live. Discuss ways students can demonstrate to their family members that they are valued.

Follow-Up/Homework Idea

- Challenge students to look for things they enjoy and appreciate about their present homes and neighborhoods.

We're moving!

Down Under Day

June 13

Setting the Stage

- Display travel brochures and posters about Australia with related literature to gather excitement about the day's activities.

- Greet your students at the door with "Good day, mate" in an Australian accent.

- Construct a semantic map or web with facts your students know (or would like to know) about Australia to help you structure the day.

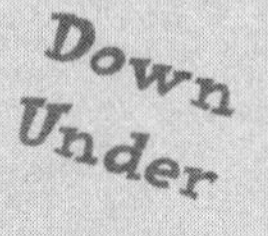

Historical Background

Although aborigines have lived in Australia as long as anyone can remember, Captain Arthur Phillip established the first permanent settlement in Sydney, Australia. His fleet of 11 ships brought more than 750 convicts from England. The prisons in England were overcrowded, so sending some convicts to Australia was an effort to relieve the problem. Today Australia is home to over 16 million people.

Literary Exploration

Australia by Donna Bailey
Australia by Peter Crawshaw
Australia by Laura Dolce
Australia by D. V. Georges
Australia by Laurence Santrey
Australia Is My Country by Bernice Moon
Australia, on the Other Side of the World by Panny Stanley-Baker
The Australian Echidna by Eleanor Stodart
The Bunyip of Berkley's Creek by Jenny Wagner
Charlie Needs a Cloak by Tomie dePaola
Down Under: Vanishing Cultures Series by Jan Reynolds
Dreamtime: Aboriginal Stories by Oodgeroo
The Flying Emu and Other Australian Stories by Sally Morgan
Joey Runs Away by Jack Kent
Joey: The Story of a Baby Kangaroo by Hope Ryden
Kangaroo by Caroline Arnold
Kangaroos on Location by Kathy Darling
Katy No-Pocket by Emmy Payne
Koala by Martha Olson Condit
Koala Lou by Mem Fox
Let's Visit Australia by John C. Caldwell
Mulga Bill's Bicycle by A. B. Paterson
My Farm by Alison Lester
Norma Jean, Jumping Bean by Joanna Cole
One Wooly Wombat by Rod Trinca and Kerry Argent
Play Ball, Joey Kangaroo by Donna Lugg
Possum Magic by Mem Fox
Punga: The Goddess of Ugly by Deborah Mourse Lattimore
Rainbow Bird: An Aboriginal Folktale from Northern Australia
   by Eric Maddern
Strange Animals of Australia by Toni Eugene
Tasmania: A Wildlife Journey by Joyce Powzyk
Where the Forest Meets the Sea by Jeannie Baker
Wombat Stew by Marcia K. Vaughan

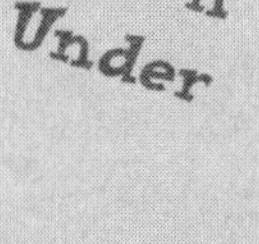

Language Experience

• Teach your students a little "Aussie lingo"!

            mate—friend
            bloke—person
            Aussie—Australian
            sheila—girl
            nipper—small child
            tucker—food
            biscuits—cookies
            bonza—good

Math Experience

- After reading Judith Viorst's *Alexander and the Terrible, Horrible, No Good, Very Bad Day* (a story in which a little boy decides he'll move to Australia), let students participate in a survey of where they would like to move when they are feeling bad. They can add this information to a class bar graph.

- If students make boomerangs today (see page 97), they can measure the distance their boomerangs traveled.

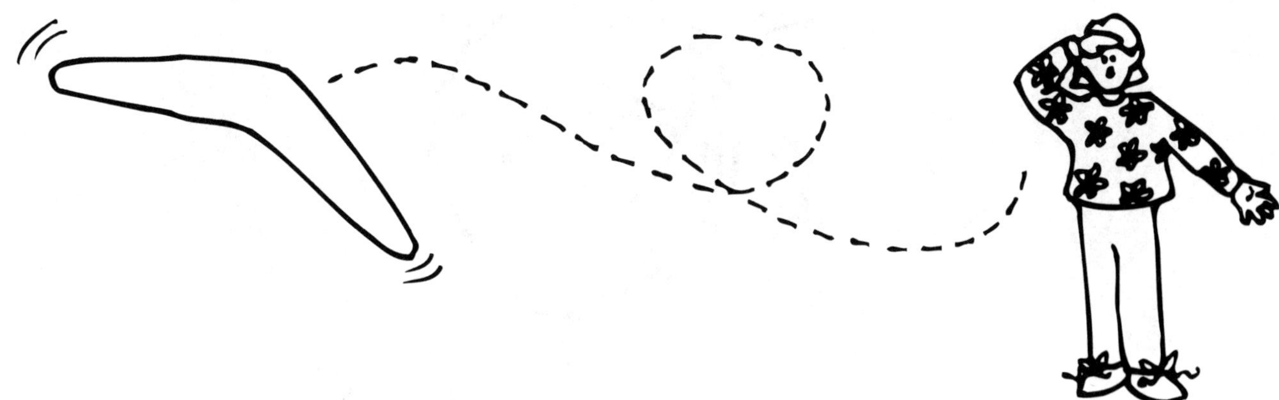

Science/Health Experience

- Your students can research unusual animals found in Australia (kangaroo, koala bear, wallaby, wombat, dingo, platypus, Tasmanian devil, emu). Have them find out which of these animals can be found only in Australia.

Social Studies Experience

• Study the continent of Australia and the interesting things that make it unique. Have students locate it on a globe. Discuss the difference between the Northern Hemisphere and the Southern Hemisphere. Show them the equator and talk about temperatures in various areas of the world.

Music/Dramatic Experience

• Australia's unofficial anthem, "Waltzing Matilda," is explained in the book called *Waltzing Matilda* by A.B. Paterson. Contrary to what many think, this song is not about a dancing woman. A "matilda" is a kind of backpack and *waltzing* means "to travel on foot."

Physical/Sensory Experience

• Younger students may enjoy jumping like kangaroos.

• If students make boomerangs today (see page 97), let them fly their boomerangs in a teacher-directed and safety-monitored area.

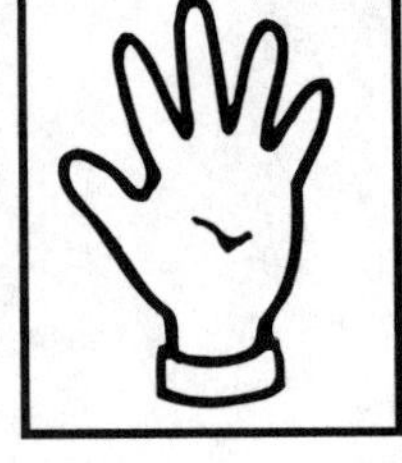

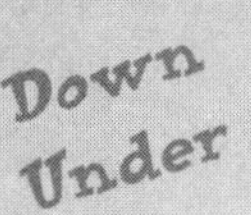

Arts/Crafts Experience

- Students can design travel posters encouraging people to visit the "Island Continent," Australia.

- Aborigines of Australia are known for their boomerangs, part of their culture and art. The boomerangs are predominantly colored red, yellow, white and black. Let students make boomerangs from tagboard to experiment with. See patterns for boomerang on page 98.

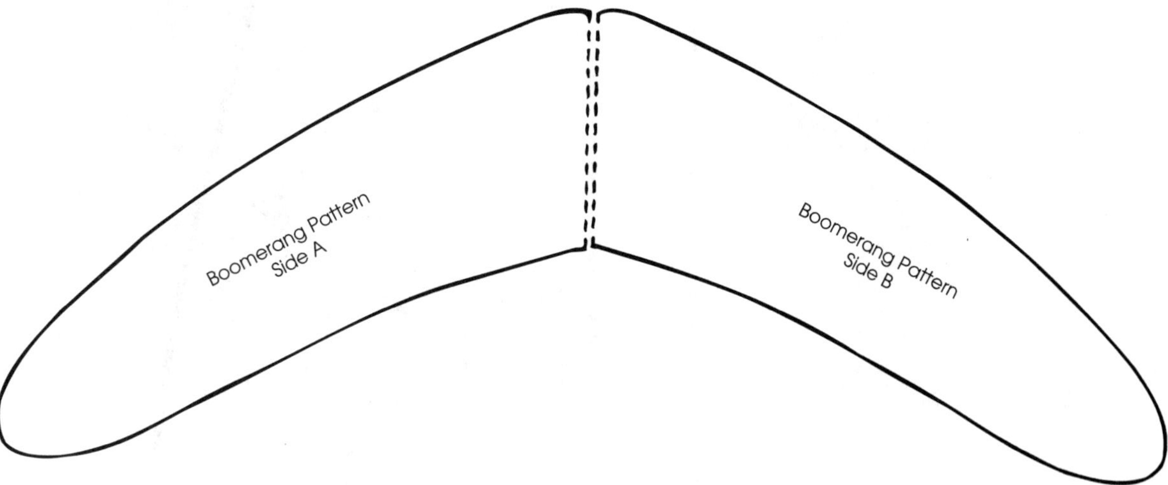

- Provide circular shapes for students to fold in half. On the top they can write *January in the Northern Hemisphere* and draw a wintry picture. On the bottom half they can write *January in the Southern Hemisphere* and draw summer activities. This is a great way for students to see in concrete terms how things are different at the same time but in different parts of the world. See pattern on page 99.

Follow-Up/Homework Idea

- Encourage students to go home and say "Good day" to their family members.

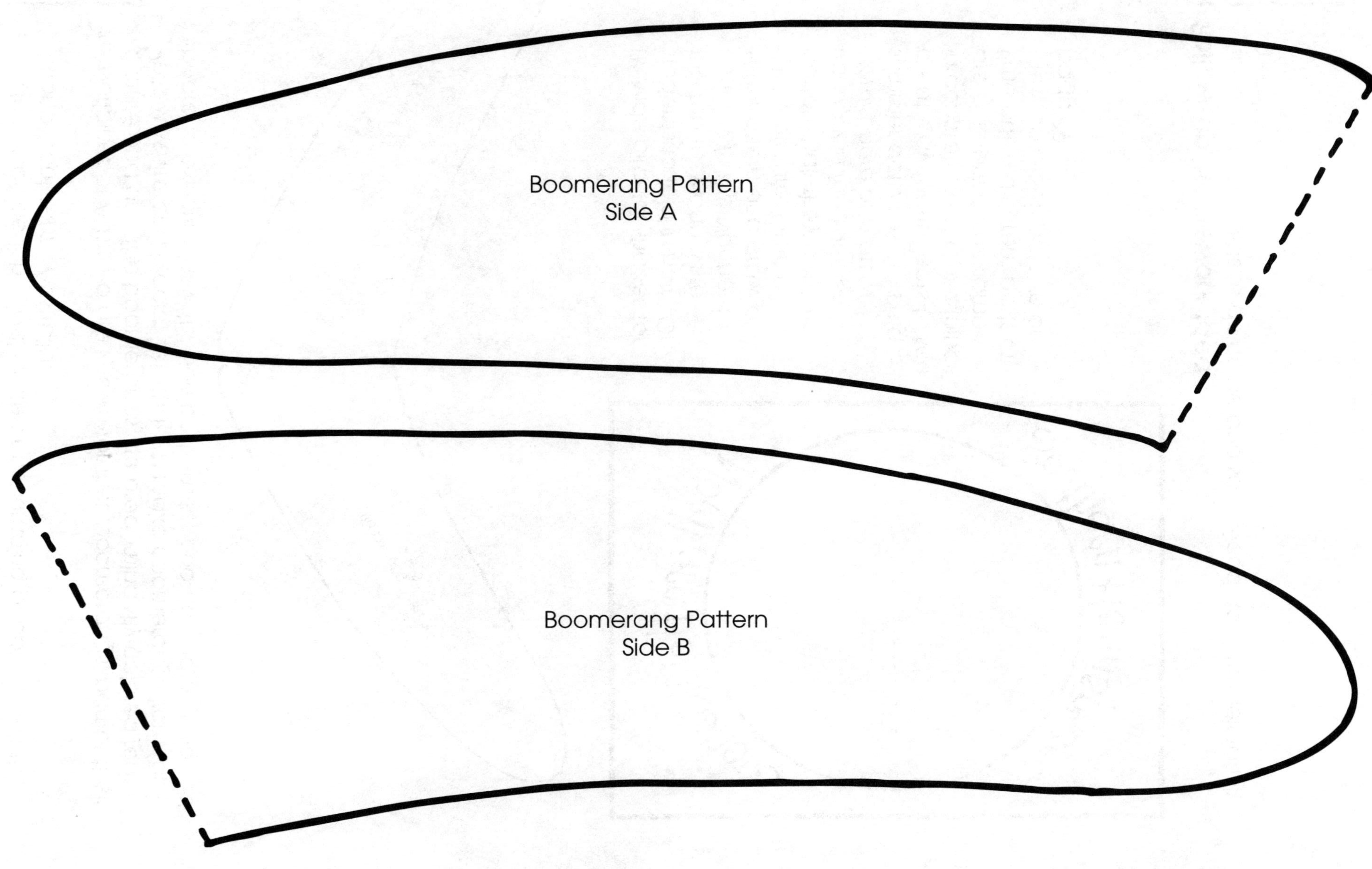

Boomerang Pattern
Side A
Boomerang Pattern
Side B

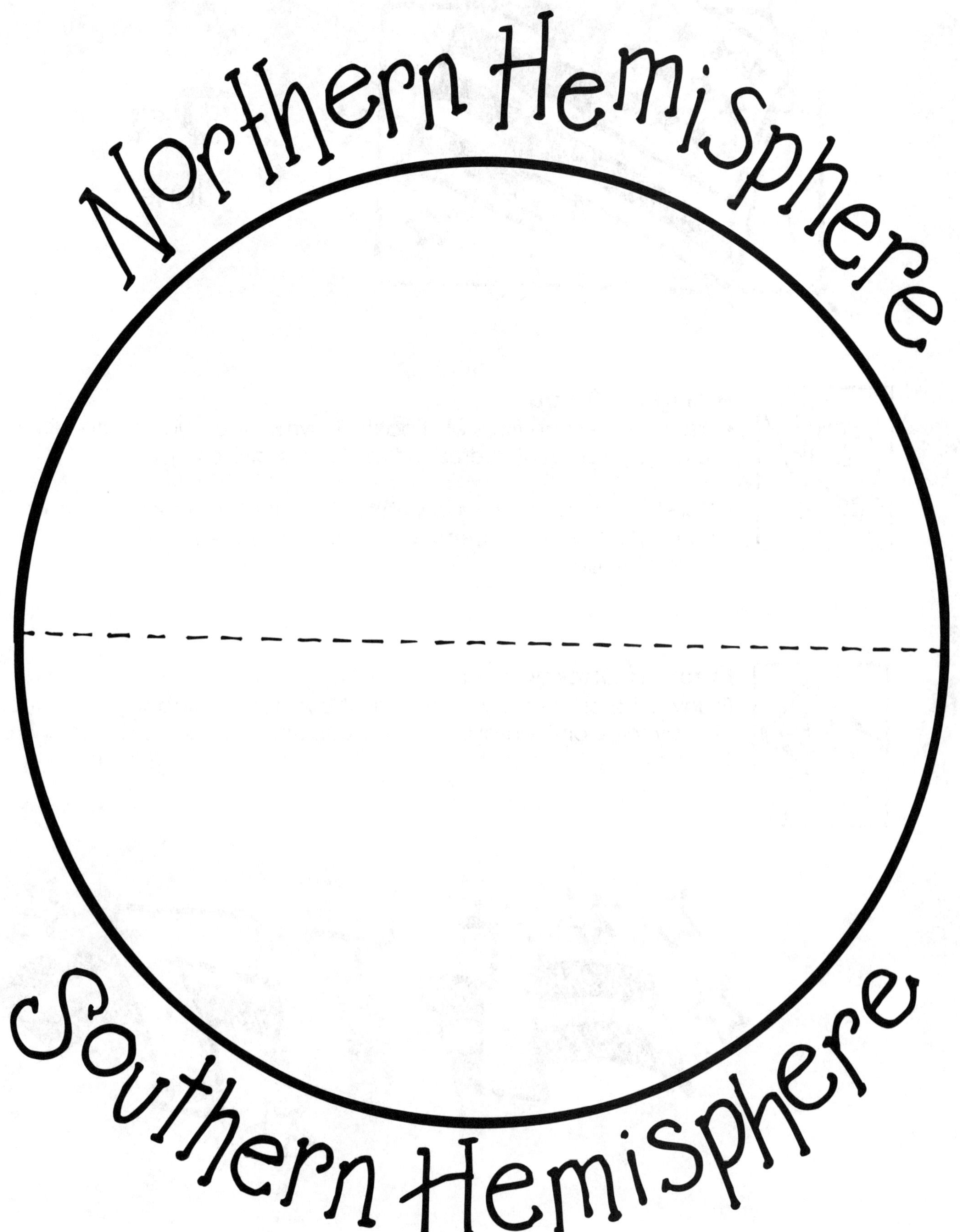

Northern Hemisphere
Southern Hemisphere

Flag Day

June 14

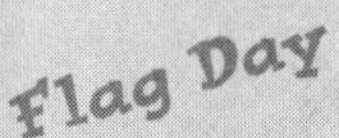

Setting the Stage

• Display American flags and patriotic symbols around related literature to engage student interest in the day's activities.

• Construct a semantic web with facts your students know about your country's flag. Invite them to list questions they would like answered during the day.

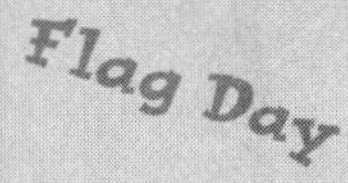

Historical Background

Today is the anniversary of the day the American flag was adopted in 1777 by the Continental Congress. Back then it had 13 stripes and only 13 stars.

Literary Exploration

The American Flag by Thomas Parrish
Betsy Ross and the Flag by Jane Mayer
Betsy Ross: Designer of Our Flag by Ann Weil
The Biggest (and Best) Flag That Ever Flew by Rebecca Jones
Flag Day by Dorothy Les Tina
Let's Find Out About Our Flag by Martha and Charles Shapp
A New Flag for Our Country by June Behrens
Our Country's Story by Frances Cavanah
Our Flag by Leslie Waller
Stars and Stripes, Our National Flag by Leonard Everett Fisher
The Star-Spangled Banner by Peter Spier
What You Should Know About the American Flag by Earl Williams
You're a Grand Old Flag by Maryjane Hooper Tonne
Your Flag and Mine by Alice Desmond

Language Experience

- See how many words your students can come up with that rhyme with *flag*.

Writing Experience

- Encourage students to write to express their feelings about the American flag. See pattern on page 105.

Social Studies Experience

- Study the history of the American flag and its symbolism.

- Find pictures of early American flags and discuss the evolution of the flag we honor. Students might want to make a time line with the dates of significant changes to the flag.

- Say the Pledge of Allegiance and discuss the meaning of the words.

- Explain how we honor the flag and the measures we take to show respect to it as our country's symbol.

Music/Dramatic Experience

- Sing "The Star-Spangled Banner" or "You're a Grand Old Flag." Discuss how and when the words to "The Star-Spangled Banner" were written by Francis Scott Key.

- Play patriotic music quietly in the background while the students are working.

Physical/Sensory Experience

• Let a student carry the American flag in a class patriotic parade marching around the classroom or school.

Arts/Crafts Experience

• Students can make tissue paper flag mosaics by tearing tiny pieces of colored tissue paper, wadding them, then gluing them to a flag background.

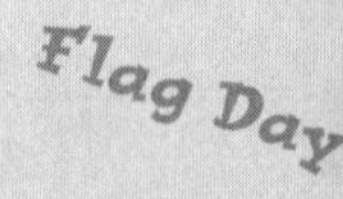

Extension Activities

- Invite some local Boy Scouts to hold a flag ceremony in your classroom.

⚠ Serve patriotic cupcakes with white frosting and miniature flags stuck on top.

⚠ Make Jelly Flags! Have each student flatten three slices of bread for a flag. They can cover the bread with jelly (nice and thick all the way to the edges). Then they stack the slices on top of each other and trim the crusts. They slice the bread into four strips and turn them on their sides to make a flag.

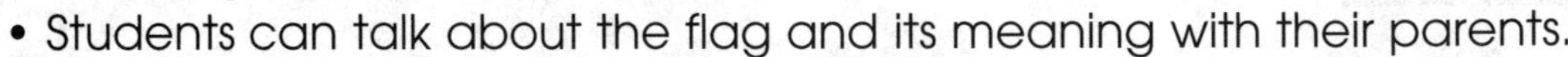

Follow-Up/Homework Idea

- Students can talk about the flag and its meaning with their parents.

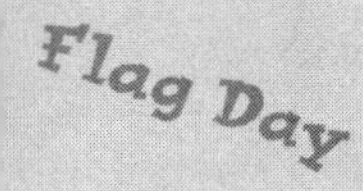

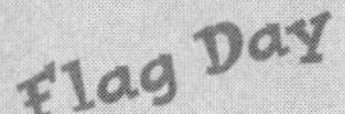

when I see the
FLAG...

Electricity Day

June 15

Setting the Stage

• Display objects that use electricity with related literature.

• Construct a semantic web with facts your students know (or would like to know) about electricity.

Historical Background

Benjamin Franklin proved lightning was a form of electricity in 1752. During a kite experiment in a lightning storm, he was able to conclude that lightning is actually an electrical charge.

Literary Exploration

All About Electricity by Melvin Berger
Electricity by Neil Ardley
Electricity by Mark Bailey
Electricity by Sam Epstein
Magnetism and Electricity by Robert Friedhoffer
Saving Electricity by Sam Epstein
The Young Scientist Book of Electricity by Phillip Chapman

Language Experience

• Let students brainstorm as many items as they can that use electricity.

Writing Experience

• Have students write humorous or reality-based stories about what causes thunder and lightning. See reproducible on page 110.

Science/Health Experience

• Begin a unit on static and current electricity. Discuss the relationship between electricity and magnetism.

• Review electrical safety.

Social Studies Experience

• Let students research Benjamin Franklin's experiment with electricity, then share their findings with the class.

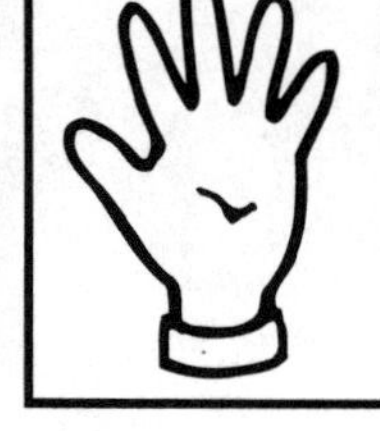

Physical/Sensory Experience

• Give your class an "electric" experience! Have students form a circle and hold hands. One squeezes another's hand, then that one passes the "squeeze" (like an electric charge) to the next person. They continue all the way around the circle. Illustrate how the charge goes in a "path." Skip a student and show how the charge cannot complete its path so it stops. Explain that a conductor (metals, water or even the human body that is made up of 70% water) gives a charge freely. A semi-conductor does not give or receive a charge as easily, but it can still be sent. An insulator, plastic, rubber or wood, is "greedy" and stops the flow of electricity.

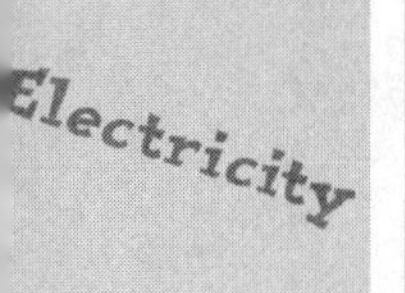
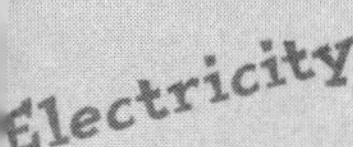

Arts/Crafts Experience
• Let students make diagrams of their homes or the classroom including things in them that use electricity.

Extension Activities
• Invite an electrician to visit your class to talk about his or her work.

Follow-Up/Homework Idea
• Encourage students to check their homes for electrical safety.

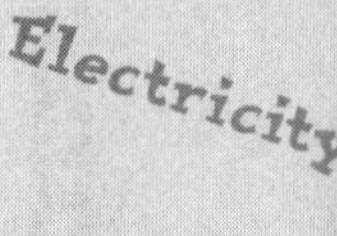

BOOM!
BOOM!
BOOM!
KABOOM

Basketball Bonanza Day

June 16

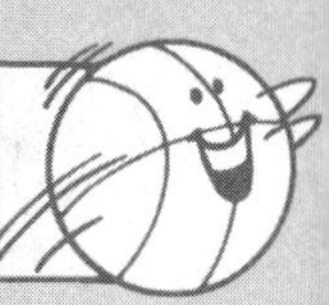
Basketball Bonanza

Setting the Stage
- Display a basketball surrounded by related literature books to get students excited about today's activities.

- Construct a semantic web with words your students think of when you say the word *basketball*.

Literary Exploration
Basketball by David Paige
Basketball by Tom Withers
The Basketball Skill Book by Earl Monroe
First Book of Basketball by Don Schiffer
I Can Read About Basketball by Richard Harris

Basketball Bonanza

Language Experience
- Play Spelling Basketball! Draw a basketball court on the board. Let students earn baskets for their teams when they correctly spell words.

Math Experience

- Go to the gym and let students measure distances from which to shoot basketballs.

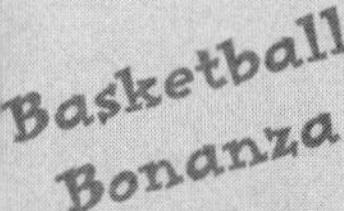

Science/Health Experience

- Review basketball safety.

- Discuss the health benefits of playing basketball.

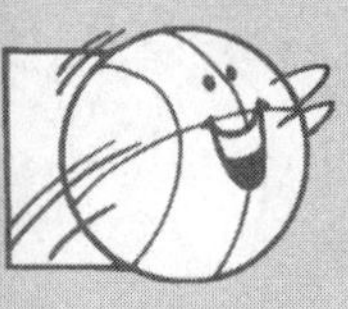

Social Studies Experience

- Learn about the history of basketball. In 1891, the winter was cold in Massachusetts. As director of the local YMCA, James Naismith was looking for a new game to play with kids indoors out of the cold. He experimented throwing a ball at two peach baskets. Of course, players had to climb a ladder after each shot to get the ball out of the basket! This made it such a slow game, they decided to cut the bottoms out of the baskets. Seven years later, the first professional basketball league was formed. Today it is the most popular indoor sport in America!

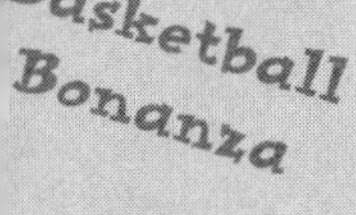

Physical/Sensory Experience

- Let students practice basic basketball skills (dribbling, passing, running).

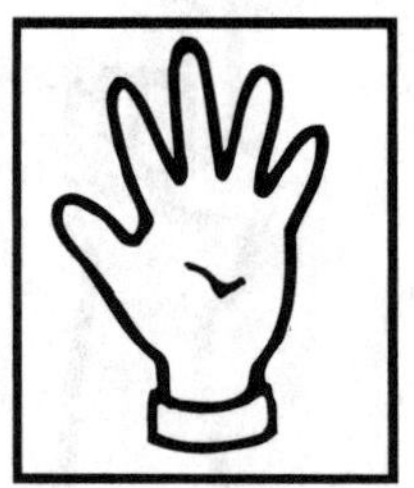

Arts/Crafts Experience

- Have students draw pictures of themselves as all-stars making the winning shot in the basketball playoffs.

Extension Activities
• Invite a local high school or college basketball player to come and talk to your class about why he or she enjoys the game of basketball, and share a few pointers on how to play the game better.

Follow-Up/Homework Idea
• Encourage students to freshen up their basketball skills with their friends or family members.

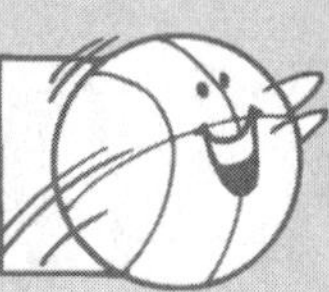

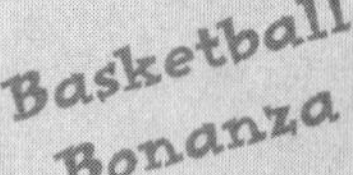

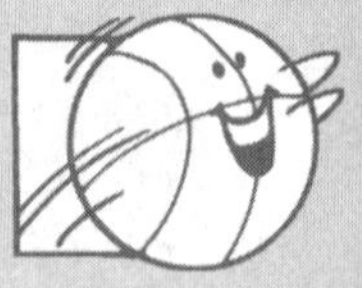

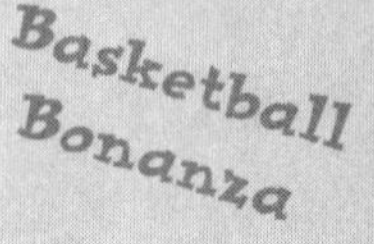

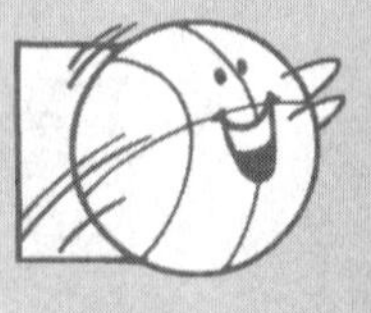

World Juggling Day

June 17

Setting the Stage

- Construct a semantic web with facts your students know about juggling. Ask them to list what they would like to learn about juggling today.

Historical Background

You probably didn't even know there was such a day, but there is . . . World Juggling Day! Jugglers all over the world teach and celebrate the art of juggling today.

Literary Exploration

How To Be a Goofy Juggler by Bruce Fife
Juggling Is for Me by Nancy Marie Temple

Language Experience

- Let each student scramble or jumble letters in a word (as if the letters were juggled in the air, but all came down mixed up). Then students can exchange papers and try to unscramble the letters to make correctly spelled words.

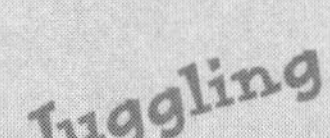

Math Experience

• Let students try juggling numbers. When adding numbers, the order is not necessarily important. Pretend you are throwing three numbers into the air (8, 3, 7). Show how the answer is the same when you add two numbers whether it's 8, 3 and 7 or 3, 8 and 7 or 7, 3 and 8.

Science/Health Experience

• As part of a healthy living unit, discuss how to "juggle" responsibilities without undue stress. What happens when we try to juggle too many things at once?

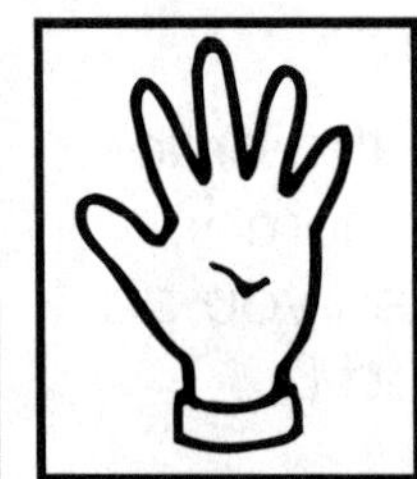

Physical/Sensory Experience

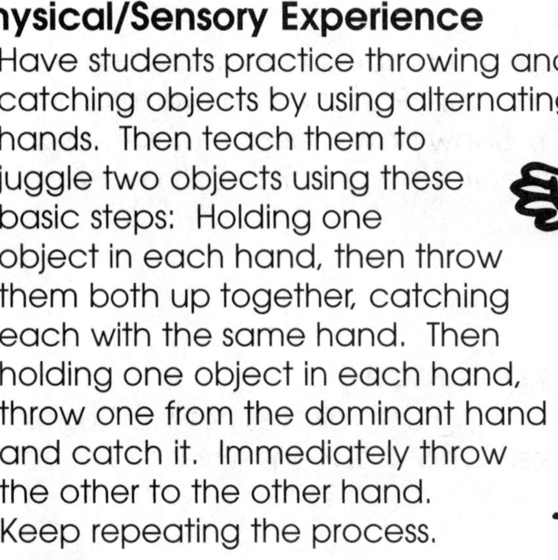

• Have students practice throwing and catching objects by using alternating hands. Then teach them to juggle two objects using these basic steps: Holding one object in each hand, then throw them both up together, catching each with the same hand. Then holding one object in each hand, throw one from the dominant hand and catch it. Immediately throw the other to the other hand. Keep repeating the process.

Extension Activities

• Invite a local juggler to come and demonstrate the techniques of juggling for your students.

Follow-Up/Homework Idea

• Encourage students to show off their new juggling talent (with unbreakable objects) to their families.

Mystery Madness Day

June 18

Setting the Stage

- Set up a display with mystery books and magnifying glasses with the caption:, "Solve a Mystery!" or "Looking for Clues to a Good Mystery?"

- Place black construction paper footprints leading into your classroom. Dress up as a secret agent or detective with trench coat, hat with wide brim, dark sunglasses and a magnifying glass to greet your students in a whispering voice.

Literary Exploration

The Dog Food Caper by Joan Lexau
Encyclopedia Brown (series) by Donald J. Sobol
The Great Brain (series) by John D. Fitzgerald
Harriet, the Spy by Louise Fitzhugh
The Hideout by Eve Bunting
Is Anybody There? by Eve Bunting
Meg MacKintosh and the Case of the Missing Babe Ruth Baseball
   by Lucinda Landon
Mousekin's Mystery by Edna Miller
The Westing Game by Ellen Raskin

Language Experience

- Play Spelling Detective! Students list their spelling words, placing one wrong letter in place of a correct one. They exchange papers and try to "detect" the missing letter and solve the spelling "crime."

- Students can make up secret codes to try to stump one another. Remind them to include a code key. (Example: * = A, # = B)

- Study mysteries as a literary genre.

Writing Experience

- Have students write letters to Sherlock Holmes asking for his help in solving something that has been a mystery to them (What happened to the missing piece of chocolate cake in the refrigerator?). See reproducible on page 122.

Math Experience

- Give students math problems with answers on the page, some of them wrong. Students must be "math detectives" and find the wrong answers.

Science/Health Experience

- Review science or health-related topics covered throughout the year with this fun guessing game: Who-Dun-It or What-Dun-It? Divide students into teams and see who can answer the most questions about scientists, inventors, inventions and scientific discoveries.

Social Studies Experience

- Assign secret pals to students to do anonymous acts of kindness for one another throughout the day. They can leave unsigned cards. At the end of the day, let students guess who their "mystery" pals were. See patterns for cards on page 123.

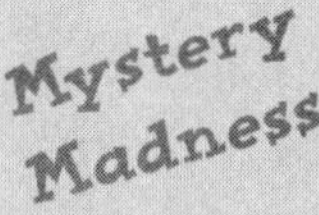

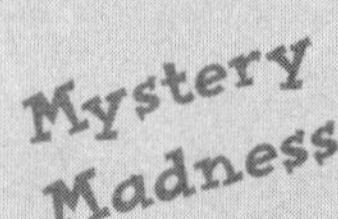

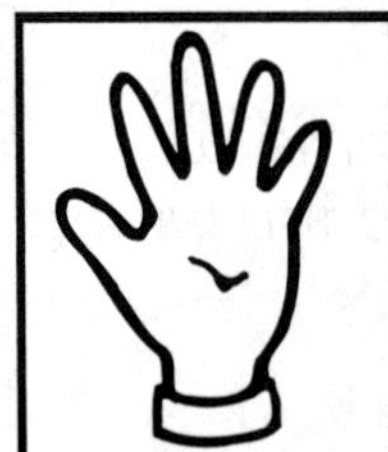

Physical/Sensory Experience

• Play I Spy! The leader picks an object in the room and gives clues so students can try to guess what it is.

• Play Mystery Box! Pull several objects out of a box and tell students to try and memorize the items. Then put them back and see how many objects the students can recall on a piece of paper.

• Students will enjoy playing Detective. Choose two students to be detectives and leave the room. Another student hides somewhere in the room while the rest switch places. The detectives come back into the room and try to identify who is missing.

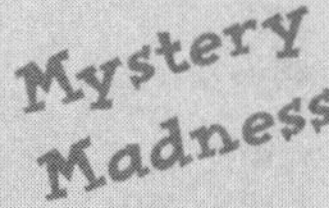

Arts/Crafts Experience

- Let students write invisible messages with lemon juice and cotton swabs. To read the messages, they hold their papers near a light bulb, but not too close.

- Students can create mystery pictures with white crayon, then paint over them and all will be revealed!

Extension Activities

- Send students on a mystery trail! Leave a set of clues at several places around the school. Students go from one clue to the next until they reach a designated destination.

⚠ Serve Mystery Pudding. Put chocolate pudding in clear plastic cups with a buried chocolate "kiss" inside each one.

Follow-Up/Homework Idea

- Encourage students to be Earth-Friendly Detectives at home, looking around and in the home for things they can do to help save the Earth's resources. (Examples: dripping faucets, trash, ways to recycle, reduce or reuse things around the house.)

Look close...
...your
Secret Pal
was here!

Look close...
...your
Secret Pal
was here!

Look close...
...your
Secret Pal
was here!

Look close...
...your
Secret Pal
was here!

Look close...
...your
Secret Pal
was here!

Look close...
...your
Secret Pal
was here!

Father's Day

June 19
(varies)

Setting the Stage

- Display items and pictures that remind students of fathers (tie, fishing pole, baseball cap, etc.) around related literature to gather excitement about the day.

- Construct a semantic web with words your students think of when you say the word *father*.

Historical Background

Father's Day was first celebrated on this day in 1910, due largely to the efforts of Mrs. John Dodd. Her father had raised her and her brothers and sisters after their mother's death. After listening to a Mother's Day sermon, she felt that fathers, too, should have a special day. She spoke to her minister after the sermon and together they drew up a proposal for a day to honor fathers everywhere. Three years later the first official Father's Day was celebrated. Today, the third Sunday of June is Father's Day every year.

Literary Exploration

About Fathers at Work by Ruth Shaw Radlauer
Always My Dad by Sharon Dennis Wyeth
Gone Fishing by Earlene Long
Happy Father's Day by Steven Kroll
A Hard Day's Work by Mick Gowar
Just Me and My Dad by Mercer Mayer
The Lost Lake by Allen Say
My Dad Is Really Something by Lois Osborn
My Dad the Magnificent by Kristy Parker
My Dad: Story and Pictures by Niki Daly
My Father's Hands by Joanne Ryder
My Mom and Dad Make Me Laugh by Nick Sharatt
My Mom and Our Dad by Rose Impey
Ramona and Her Father by Beverly Cleary
The Trouble with Dad by Babette Cole
You and Your Dad by Lou Alpert
Your Dad Was Just Like You by Dolores Johnson

Language Experience

• Create a Venn diagram depicting the similarities and differences between mothers and fathers.

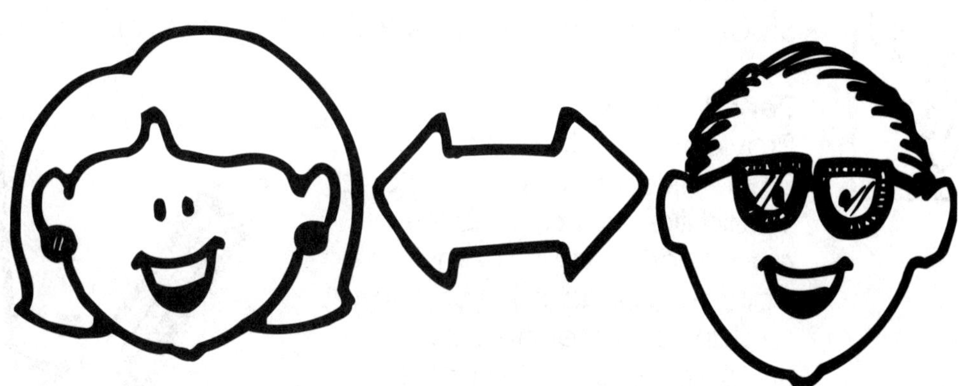

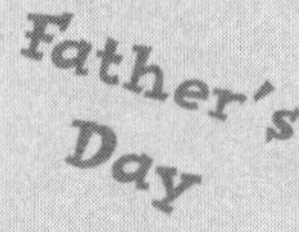

• How many words can your students come up with that rhyme with the word *dad*?

Writing Experience

- Let students write letters or poems to their fathers. See reproducible on page 128.

- Have students write "dad" stories using these story starters:

    My dad built me a tree house, but . . .

    When I went fishing with my dad, he made me laugh when . . .

    My dad is a great gardener, one year he grew . . .

    My dad loves to play golf, but he isn't very good. Once he . . .

Arts/Crafts Experience

- Students can make Father's Day gifts for their fathers.

Pencil Holder

Provide clean jars or cans. Students can cut pictures dad would like that describe their dads. They can glue them in a collage around a jar or can. A sealant of water and glue can be painted over the entire surface.

Paperweight

Follow the directions for a pencil holder but do it on a smooth, clean rock.

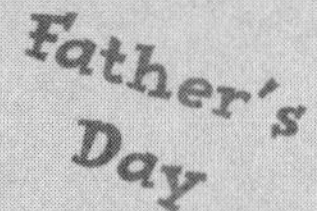

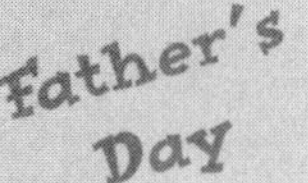

Arts/Crafts Experience continued

Special Card
Students can draw a picture of a tie on tagboard and cut it out. On the front, they can write *There is no TIE because you are the best in the whole world!*

Coupon Book
Let students make coupon books with coupons their dads can redeem for services. (Example: Breakfast in bed) See patterns on pages 129-130.

Extension Activities
⚠ Serve Father's Day Frappe! Blend milk, chocolate ice cream and chocolate syrup in a blender and serve some to each student.

• Invite students' fathers to come and talk about the rewards of being a father.

Follow-Up/Homework Idea
• Encourage students to show appreciation for their dads.

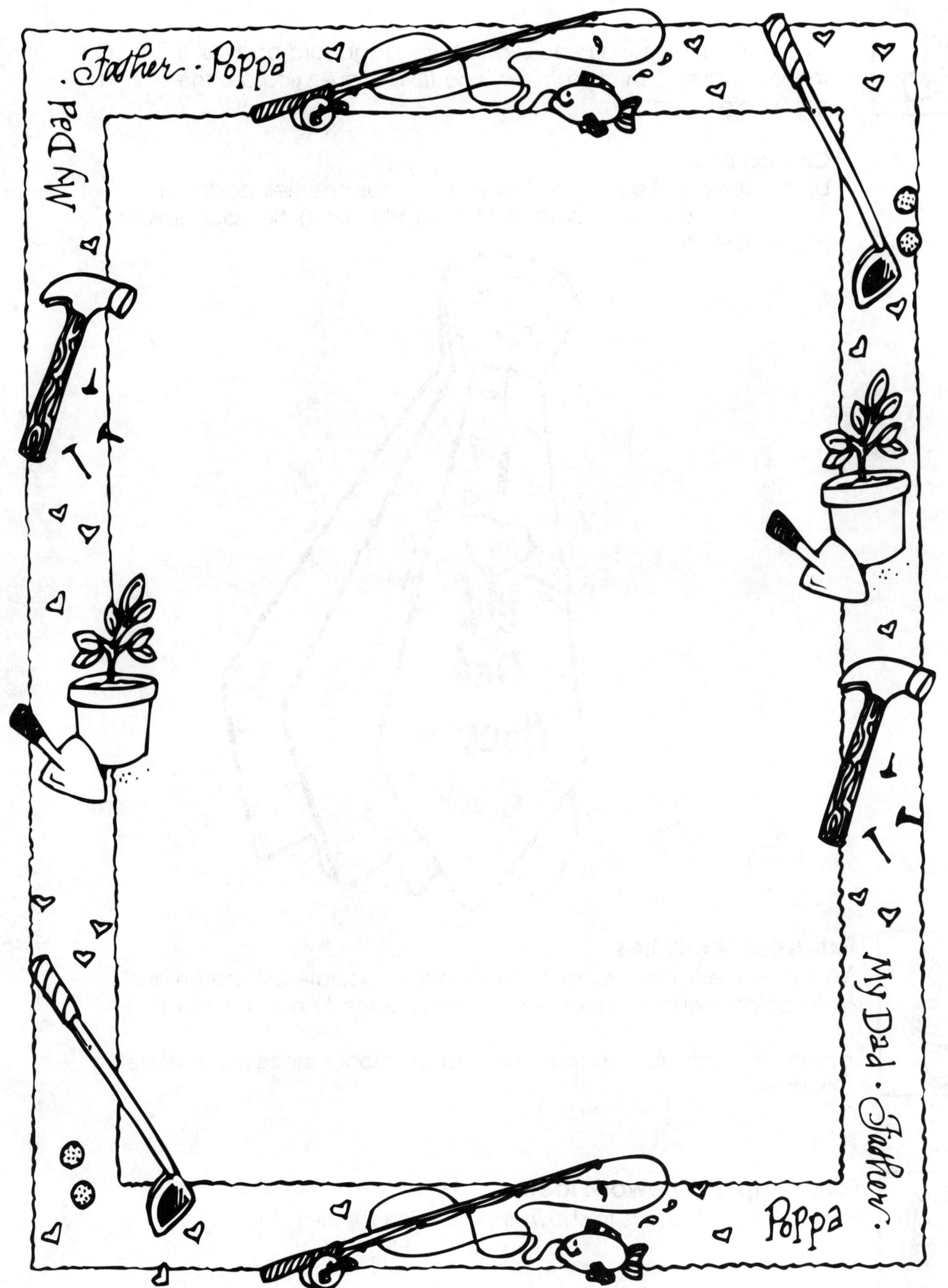

My Dad · Father · Poppa

I
love
My
Dad
Coupon
Book

Happy
Father's
Day!

To:
From:

Good
for one

Good
for one

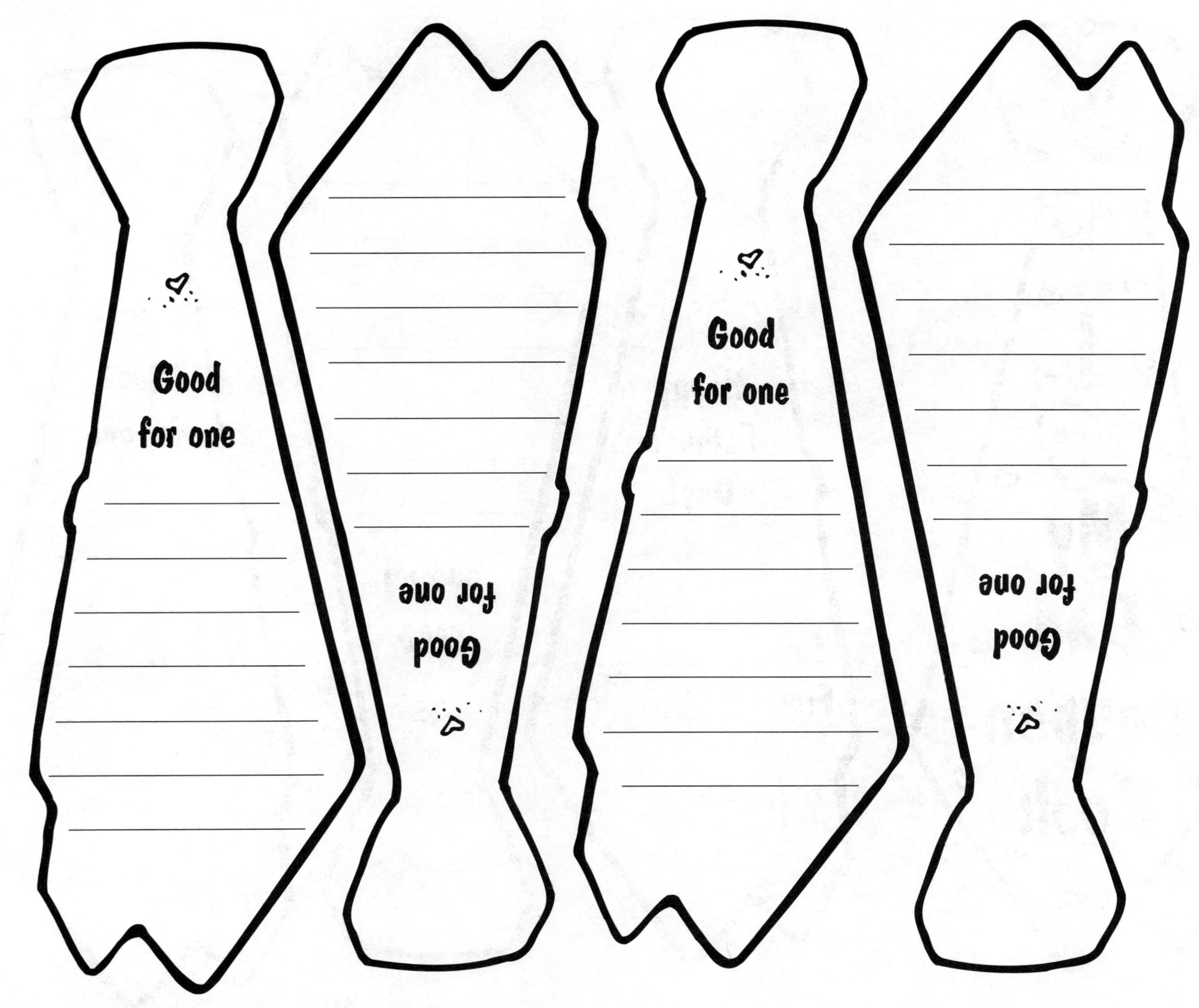

Good
for one
Good
for one
Good
for one
Good
for one

West Virginia Statehood Day

June 20

Setting the Stage
- Display literature and pictures about the state of West Virginia to engage student interest.

Historical Background
West Virginia became the 35th state in the Union on this day in 1863.

Literary Exploration
America the Beautiful: West Virginia
   by R. Conrad Stein
West Virginia by Allan Carpenter
West Virginia by Kathleen Thompson
West Virginia in Words and Pictures
   by Dennis B. Fradin

Language Experience
- How many new words can your students make using the letters in *West Virginia*?

- Have students check out the names of cities and towns in West Virginia and guess how they got their names. (Examples: Oak Hill, Mountain View, Shady Spring)

Writing Experience

- An interesting feature of West Virginia is the National Radio Astronomy Observatory. The huge discs and antennas seek signals from outer space. Have students write about a day when the instruments receive a message from outer space. What is it? How do scientists respond? Encourage students to use their imagination to write exciting stories.

- White water rafting is a popular sport in West Virginia. Let students write about an exciting raft ride with a surprising end!

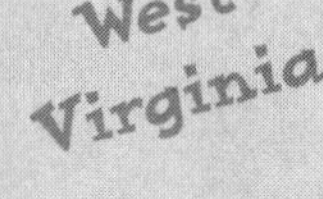

Math Experience

- Have students research to find out the current population of West Virginia, then compare it with the population of their state. How much bigger or smaller is West Virginia? (If you live in West Virginia, choose another state for comparison.)

Science/Health Experience

- West Virginia has a natural history landmark which includes huge hemlock trees. Some are 350 years old and 90 feet tall. Study trees and have students compare hemlocks with other large trees such as redwoods and sycamores.

- Have students do some research to discover some of the flowers and other kinds of plants that flourish in West Virginia.

Social Studies Experience

- Have students look at a United States map to see what five states border West Virginia.

Social Studies Experience continued

• Study the state of West Virginia and what makes it unique.

• Have students look at maps of West Virginia. Let them practice reading maps to figure out how to get from one place to another and decide about how long it will take by car.

Arts/Crafts Experience

• Let students make salt dough relief maps of West Virginia. Bake them at 325°F for an hour, then let them cool. Students can paint them.

Extension Activities

⚠ West Virginia's state tree is the sugar maple. Serve pancakes with homemade maple syrup.

Maple Syrup

Boil 2 cups of brown sugar and 1 cup of water until it begins to thicken. Add 1 teaspoon of maple flavoring and serve over pancakes.

• Invite someone who has been to West Virginia to talk about it and share pictures and souvenirs with the class.

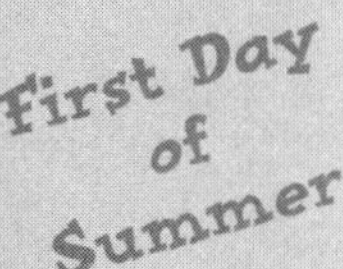

First Day of Summer

June 21

Setting the Stage

- Display student-made pictures of summer activities drawn inside the shape of a yellow sun with the caption: "Our Future Looks SUNNY!" See reproducible on page 139.

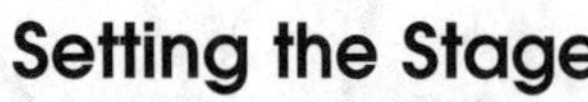

Historical Background

Traditionally, June 21st is the first day of summer in the Northern Hemisphere.

134

Literary Exploration

Anna's Summer Songs by Mary Q. Steele
City in the Summer by Eleanor Schick
The Coolest Place in Town by Kathy Caple
Cranberry Summer by Wende and Harry Devlin
Emilio's Summer Day by Miriam Anne Bourne
The Lovely Summer by Marc Simont
My Summer Vacation by Sumiko
On Vacation by Richard Scarry
Shooting Star Summer by Candice Ransom
The Sounds of Summer by David Updike
Summer by Richard Allington
Summer by Alice Low
Summer by Fiona Pragoff
Summer by Carme Sole Vendrell
Summer Business by Charles Martin
Summer: A Growing Time by Janet McDonnell
Summer Is by Charlotte Zolotow
Summer Is Here by Jane Belk Moncure
Summer Night by Charlotte Zolotow
The Summer Noisy Book by Margaret Wise Brown
Summer Story by Jill Barklem
The Twelve Days of Summer by Elizabeth Lee O'Donnell
What Ernie and Bert Did on Their Summer Vacation by Patricia Thackray
When I Was Nine by James Stevenson
When Summer Comes by Robert Maass

Language Experience

• Invite students to begin a reading challenge over the summer. Encourage them to keep track of the books and total number of pages they read each day.

• Let students brainstorm everything they would like to do this summer.

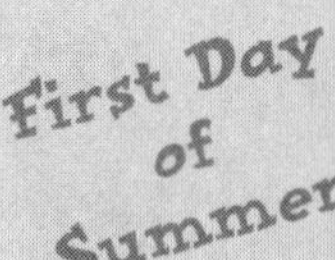

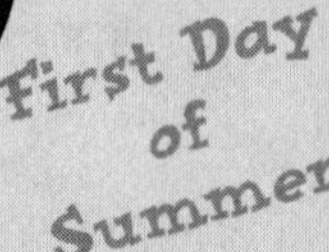

Writing Experience

- Let students write acrostic poems about summer, writing the word *SUMMER* vertically down a piece of paper, then writing a descriptive word beginning with each letter.

- Students can write about their summer vacation plans.

- Let students begin a "Summer Scrapbook of Memories." They can add a page each day throughout the summer.

- See reproducible for writing activities on page 140.

Math Experience

- Students can keep track of sunny days this summer on a tally chart.

- Have students practice addition and subtraction using garden seeds as manipulatives.

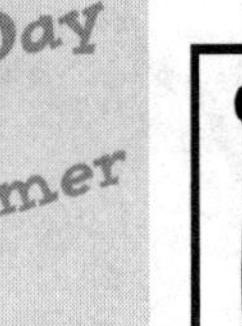

Science/Health Experience

- Review summer safety.

Music/Dramatic Experience
• Sing "Oh, What Do You Do in the Summertime?"
  by Dorothy S. Anderson.

Physical/Sensory Experience
• Play Slip and Slide Kickball! Set up a Slip and Slide™ in a grassy area
  of the playground. Set the area up around it like a baseball diamond
  with the Slip and Slide™ between third base and home plate. Set
  pails of water at first and second bases. Students can wear appropriate swimwear. Have them play kickball, but when they get to a base,
  they must step a foot in a pail of water, then slide to home base, on
  the Slip and Slide™.

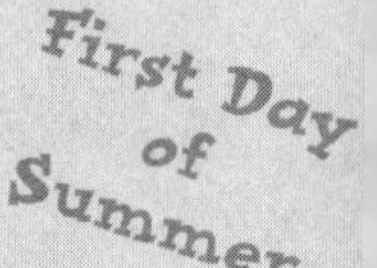

Arts/Crafts Experience

• Let students draw pictures of their favorite summer activities.

• Students can draw sidewalk murals with colored chalk on sidewalks.

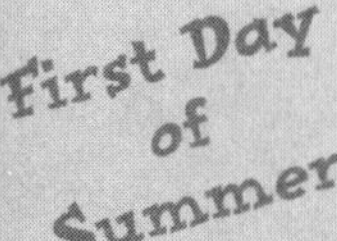

Extension Activities

⚠ Serve lemonade or homemade limeade!

Limeade

Mix three small cans of frozen lemonade with the juice of two fresh limes. Add to a bottle of ginger ale.

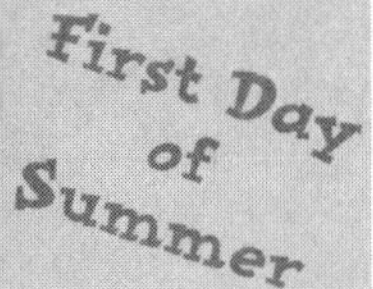

Follow-Up/Homework Idea

• Challenge students to have the best summer ever, using some of the time off to be helpful to others.

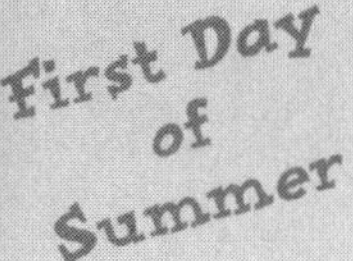

Our future looks
Sunny!

SUMMER

Spectacles Day

June 22

Setting the Stage

- Display eye paraphernalia (glasses, goggles, eye chart) around related literature.

- Construct a semantic map with facts your students know about eyes and glasses. List additional information your class wants to learn today.

Historical Background

Benjamin Franklin invented bifocals in 1784. He got tired of switching his glasses all the time, one pair for his nearsightedness and another pair for his farsightedness. So he simply took the lenses out of two pairs of glasses, cut them in half and put half of each in one frame!

Literary Exploration

Arthur's Eyes by Marc Brown
Ben's Glasses by David Johnson
Chimps Don't Wear Glasses by Laura Joffe Numeroff
Cromwell's Glasses by Holly Keller
Glasses: Who Needs 'Em? by Lane Smith
Goggles! by Ezra Jack Keats
I Need Glasses! by Angelika Wolff
Little Hippo Gets Glasses by Maryann MacDonald
Monty, the Dog Who Wears Glasses by Colin West
Mr. Turtle's Magic Glasses by Jane Thayer
Spectacles by Ellen Raskin
Why Do I Have to Wear Glasses? by Sandra Lee Stuart

Language Experience

• Let students brainstorm as many words as they can that rhyme with the word *eye*.

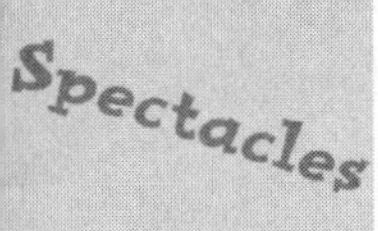

Writing Experience

• Students can write stories about a strange pair of glasses they picked up and how things changed when they put the glasses on.
See reproducible on page 147.

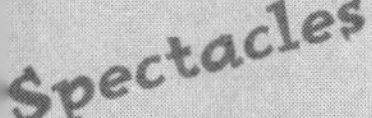

Math Experience

- Let students work together on a class bar graph showing the different eye colors of students in the room. Have them note which color is most common, least common, the total of the two added together and so on.

Science/Health Experience

- Review eye safety! Discuss safety precautions such as avoiding looking directly at the sun, wearing safety goggles around some equipment and rubbing eyes that have dirt or sand in them.

Social Studies Experience

- Study the history of eyeglasses. Roman Emperor Nero used to watch performances by holding a curved jewel in front of one eye. It is believed that he was nearsighted and holding the jewel in front of the eye helped him to see.

- The Chinese were the first to wear "glasses" as we know them. They were made with large rock crystal oval lenses in tortoise shell frames held up by two weighted cords hung over the ears or fastened to a hat. They were often worn as adornment or to bring good luck.

- Europeans were the first people we know of who wore glasses to aid eyesight. These were magnifying glasses held up to the eye by the hand. Even doctors could not see "eye to eye" on treatment for poor vision. Some doctors looked disparagingly at glasses, believing that the only way to help poor eyesight was with ointments and lotions. Time proved ointments to be ineffective and glasses grew more and more in popularity. Benjamin Franklin was credited with perfecting the glass lens with the invention of his bifocals.

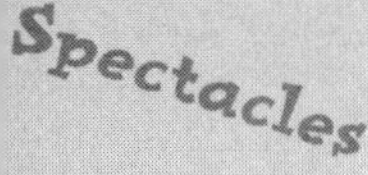

Physical/Sensory Experience

- Check out a book on optical illusions from the library and try a few experiments with your class.

Arts/Crafts Experience

- Try some bifocal art. Give students a large bifocal glasses pattern. They pick something to draw, then draw one half miniaturized and one half enlarged as viewed through a pair of bifocal lenses. See pattern on page 148.

- Students can make fun eye-glasses with two connecting sections of plastic six-pack soda pop rings. Provide two connecting sections for each student and let them add pipe cleaners for ear pieces.

Extension Activities

- Invite an ophthalmologist to come and talk to your class about his or her work.

- Visit an optometrist's office and learn how they help people see better.

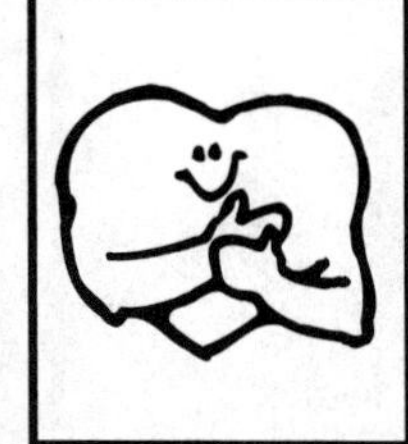

Values Education Experience

- Discuss what it means to "see" with your eyes, and to "see" with your heart.

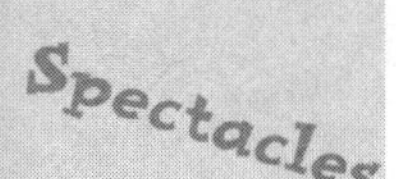

Follow-Up/Homework Idea

- Encourage students to share what they learned about vision care and eye safety with their families.

146

What do "eye" see?

Rainbow Appreciation Day

June 23

Setting the Stage

• Invite students to wear their favorite colors today!

• Construct a semantic web with words your students think of when you say the word *rainbow*.

Literary Exploration

Brown Bear, Brown Bear, What Do You See? by Bill Martin
Calico Cat Looks at Colors by Donald Charles
Color by Ruth Heller
Color Dance by Ann Jonas
A Color of His Own by Leo Lionni
The Great Blueness and Other Predictaments by Arnold Lobel
Hailstones and Halibut Bones by Mary O'Neill
Little Blue and Little Rainbow by Leo Lionni
Peony's Rainbow by Martha Weston
Planting a Rainbow by Lois Ehlert
Rainbow Bird: An Aboriginal Folktale from Northern Australia
  by Eric Madden
The Rainbow Fish by Marcus Pfister
A Rainbow of My Own by Don Freeman
Rainbow Rhino by Peter Sis
Skyfire by Frank Asch
Swinging on a Rainbow by Charles Perkins
The Tale of the Vanishing Rainbow by Siegfried Rupprecht
Tom's Rainbow Walk by Catherine Anholt
Who Said Red? by Mary Serfozo

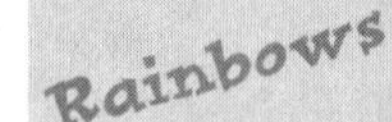

Language Experience

• Let students each choose a color, then brainstorm as many things as they can that could be that color.

Writing Experience

• After reading *Hailstones and Halibut Bones* by Mary O'Neill, let students each write about a certain color and the things that come to mind with that particular color. (Example: Yellow looks like the sun or tastes like sour lemon drops.) See pattern on page 154.

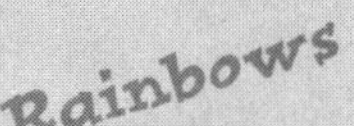

150

Math Experience

• Make a class bar graph of the colors students see outside your classroom window.

Science/Health Experience

• Try making an indoor rainbow. Simply fill a roasting pan with water and place it in a sunny spot in your room. Place a small mirror at an angle halfway in the water. Make sure the sunlight hits the mirror. The water acts like a prism, splitting the light into colors like a raindrop would. Watch the ceiling for the rainbow!

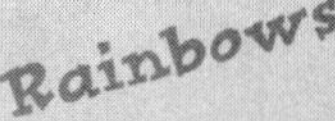

Music/Dramatic Experience

• Sing with your little "munchkins" "Somewhere over the Rainbow" written by E.Y. Harburg. Two other color song favorites are "Sing a Rainbow" by Arthur Hamilton and "The Little Blue Man" by Fred Ebb and Paul Klein.

Physical/Sensory Experience

• Give students different colors of tissue paper and put on "colorful" music. They can do creative dance and shake the colored tissue in the air.

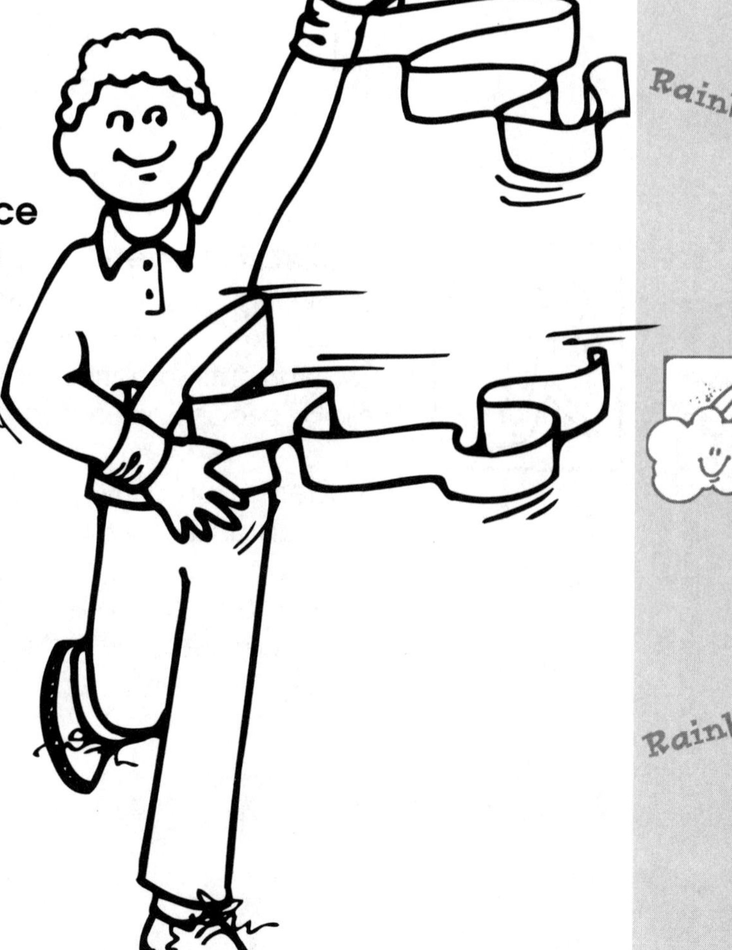

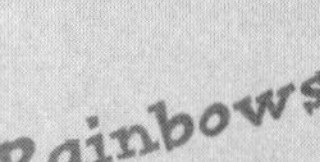

Physical/Sensory Experience continued

• Do you have leftover colored tissue or construction paper scraps going to waste? Students can practice categorizing colors and help save the Earth's resources at the same time. Provide a different container for each color. As students have leftover scraps of colored paper they can place them in the appropriate containers. Then as the need arises, the scraps can be used first.

• Invite students to make a rainbow (with the colors of the spectrum) by the clothes they are wearing. They can divide themselves into color groups, then arrange themselves in appropriate rainbow color order.

Arts/Crafts Experience

• Study which colors are warm, which are cool and which are neutrals.

• Let students experiment with colors. Have them mix primary colors to make secondary colors or neutrals such as brown.

• Students can draw pictures of natural colors found in plants, birds, animals and other parts of the natural world.

• Let students paint their own rainbows in the seven colors of the spectrum: red, orange, yellow, green, blue, indigo and violet.

Extension Activities

⚠ Serve rainbow treats. Introduce one color at a time and let students eat something of that color. (Examples: chocolate pudding, orange slices, black licorice, white marshmallows, grape juice or fresh purple grapes, green grapes or Jell-O™, blueberry muffins, lemon drops or lemonade, red cinnamon candies, strawberries or apples.

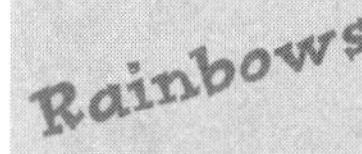

Values Education Experience

• Discuss what the world would be like without color. We should appreciate our colorful world and not take it for granted.

Follow-Up/Homework Idea

• Encourage your students to notice the beautiful colors in their yards and neighborhoods.

Yellow
Red
White
Green
Brown
Orange
Blue
Black
Purple

Theme Park Day

June 24

Setting the Stage

- Display pictures of famous amusement parks (like Disneyland) to the not-so-famous (local carnivals) around related literature to gather excitement in today's activities.

Historical Background

Disneyland, America's first theme park, opened in California in the summer of 1955. Since then theme parks have popped up all over the country.

Literary Exploration

Behind the Scenes of the Amusement Park by Elizabeth Van Steenwyk
Carousel by Donald Crews
Curious George Visits an Amusement Park by Margret Rey

Language Experience

- Let students brainstorm words that have the "ar" sound as in the word *park*.

Writing Experience

- Ask students to imagine that a famous amusement park needs a new idea for a theme ride. Have them write their proposals for new rides. See reproducible on page 158.

- Let students imagine that they are spending the day with friends at a theme park. Have them write about their experiences, using lots of vibrant adjectives to describe what they see and do.

- Challenge students to write rhyming poems about an amusement park as an advertisement to make people want to come there. Before they begin writing, take a few minutes to brainstorm rhyming words that they can use. (Examples: fun, run, sun, none; ride, slide, inside, hide, glide; eat, meet, treat, neat; yummy, tummy, chummy)

Math Experience

- Hand out play money and lists of amusement park prices, then ask students to work in pairs, one person acting as the park "clerk" and the other as the visitor who has to pay. Create problems for them to work out. (Example: You want to ride the roller coaster—50¢, then get some popcorn—25¢ and a soda—50¢. How much will it cost? How much change will the clerk give you if you pay him or her $2? $5?

- Ask students to take a survey of other students' favorite amusement parks. Then add this information to a class bar graph.

Science/Health Experience

- Review amusement park safety (holding onto metal bars, staying with friends, avoiding too much junk food, etc.).

Social Studies Experience

- Study the history of amusement parks. Your students will be interested to know that amusement parks date back all the way to the seventeenth century. Discuss the similarities and differences between amusement parks and theme parks.

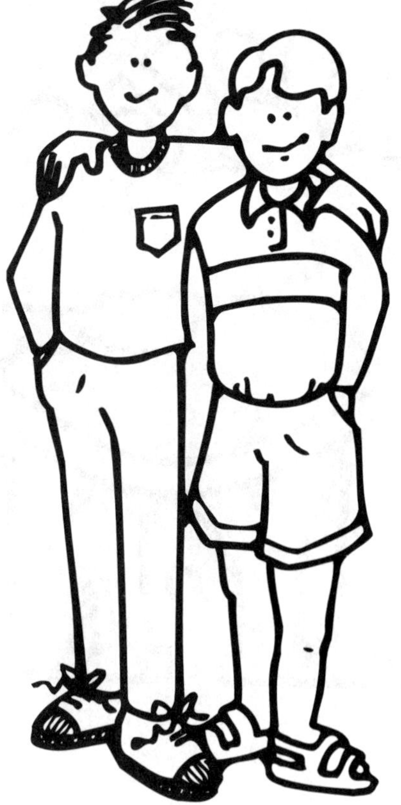

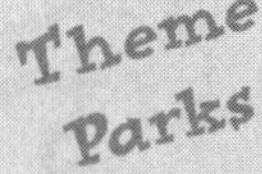

Arts/Crafts Experience

- Let each student draw a design for a new theme park in your town.

- Have students create a new mascot for a theme park and name it.

Extension Activities

- Invite a guest from a local amusement park to visit your class to talk about his or her work.

Follow-Up/Homework Idea

- Encourage students to create a neighborhood theme park with their friends (simple rides, petting zoo, music and food).

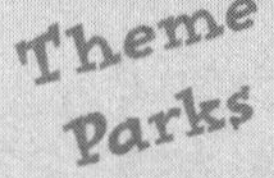

MY·NEW·RIDE

Eric Carle's Birthday

June 25

Setting the Stage
- Display Eric Carle's books with several pieces of fruit or stuffed animals from his stories.

Historical Background
Children's author, Eric Carle, celebrates his birthday today!

Literary Exploration
1, 2, 3 to the Zoo by Eric Carle
All About Arthur by Eric Carle
Do You Want to Be My Friend? by Eric Carle
Eric Carle's Animals, Animals by Eric Carle
Eric Carle's Storybook by Eric Carle
The Grouchy Ladybug by Eric Carle
Have You Seen My Cat? by Eric Carle
A House for a Hermit Crab by Eric Carle
The Hungry Caterpillar by Eric Carle
I See a Song by Eric Carle
Let's Paint a Rainbow by Eric Carle
The Mixed-Up Chameleon by Eric Carle
My Apron: A Story from My Childhood by Eric Carle
My Very First Book of Food by Eric Carle
My Very First Book of Numbers by Eric Carle
My Very First Book of Shapes by Eric Carle
Pancakes, Pancakes by Eric Carle
Papa, Please Get the Moon for Me by Eric Carle

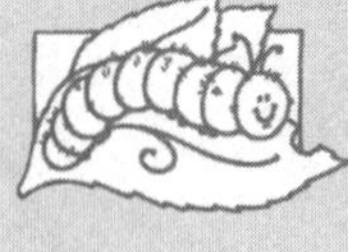

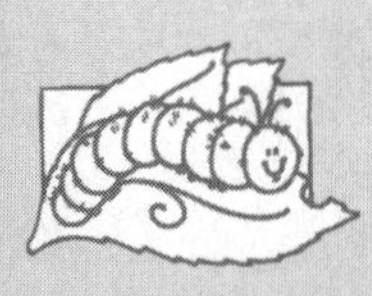

Literary Exploration continued

The Tiny Seed by Eric Carle
Today Is Monday by Eric Carle
The Very Busy Spider by Eric Carle
The Very Lonely Firefly by Eric Carle
The Very Quiet Cricket by Eric Carle
Walter the Baker by Eric Carle

Language Experience

• Review story sequencing with your students with the fruit (in order of appearance) in the story of *The Hungry Caterpillar*. This is also a great opportunity to review compound words (watermelon, butterfly, strawberries) or syllabication, having students clap out syllables in words such as: *caterpillar, cocoon* and *pickle*.

Writing Experience

• Review plurals and encourage creativity by letting students make Hungry Caterpillar books! They can pattern their books after the original being careful to include a single piece of food on the first page ("On Monday, the hungry caterpillar ate one carrot"). Point out that this is the only time in the story that food is in a singular mode. As the pages progress, students need to add new food items in plural form ("three radishes, eight cucumbers"). Young students sometimes forget to use the plural form where needed, so this book provides a great opportunity for reinforcement.

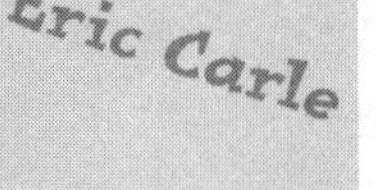

Math Experience

• Let students follow the pattern of Eric Carle's book, *My Very First Book of Numbers,* to create number books for themselves or younger students.

Science/Health Experience

• After reading Eric Carle's book, *The Hungry Caterpillar,* talk about good nutrition.   Teach students to choose nutritious foods (using a Food Guide Pyramid). Help them learn how many servings of each kind of food they need every day. Let them make their own pyramids, drawing or cutting food pictures from magazines to go in each area of the pyramid.

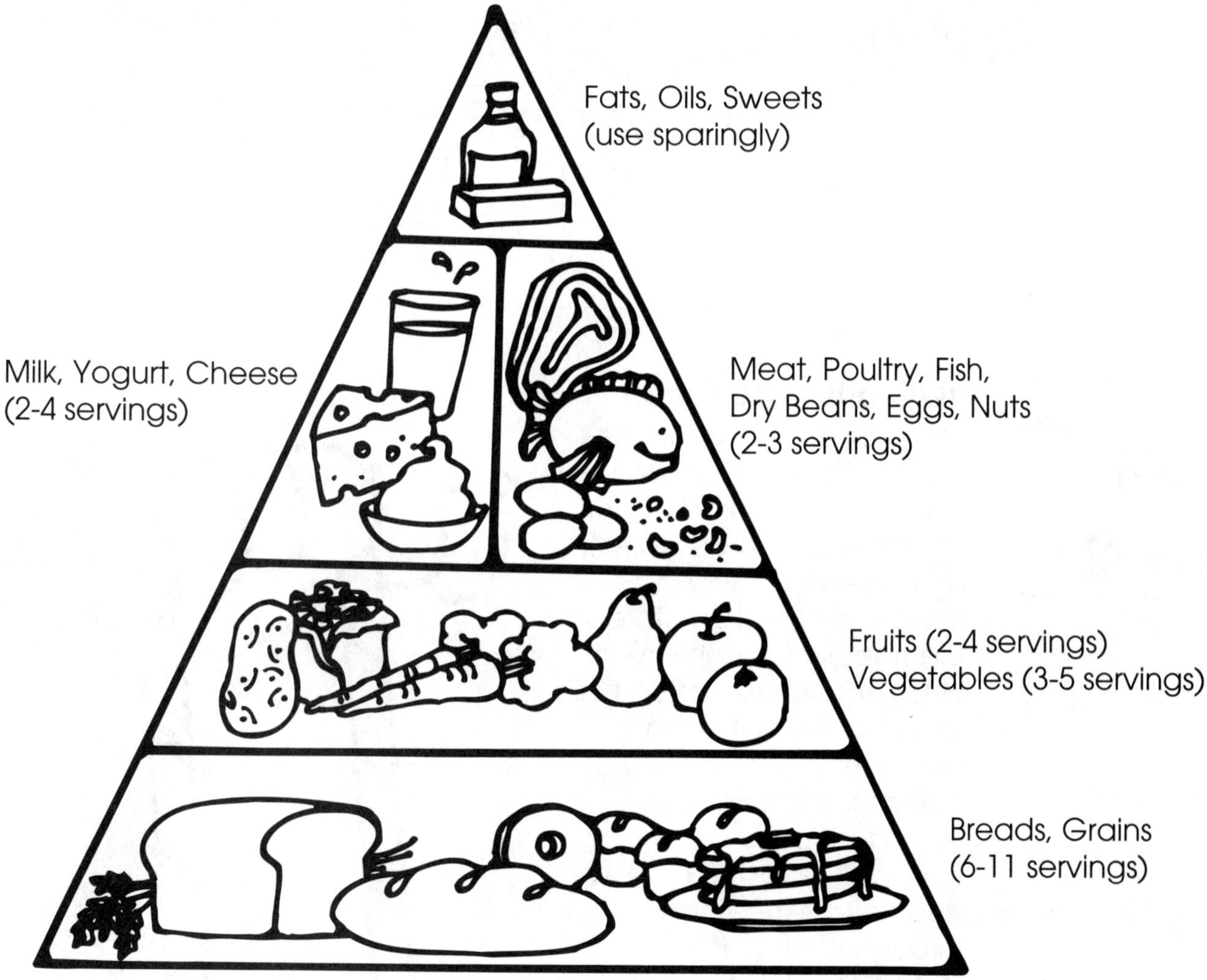

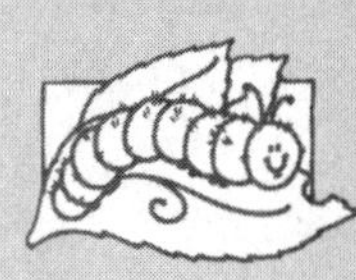
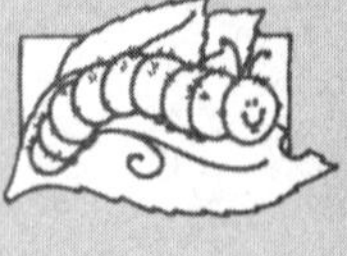
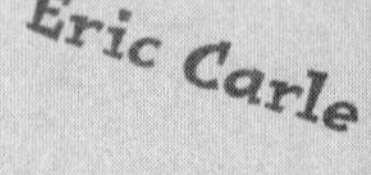

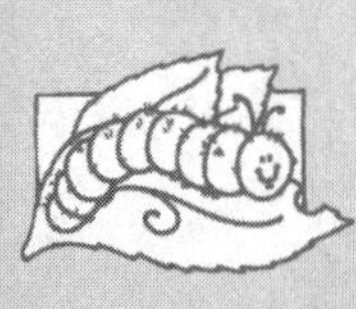
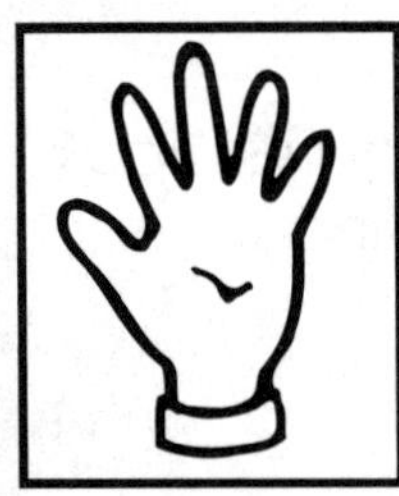
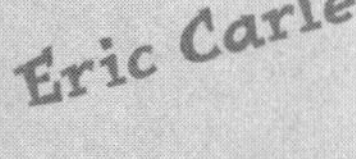

Physical/Sensory Experience

• Play Bingo with food! Give each student raisins for markers and a Bingo card. Divide students into groups of eight or less so a winner from each group can be determined. Instead of calling out each food, give clues such as: This is round and the color says its name. It is sweet and juicy! When a student finds five nutritious foods in a row, he or she calls out "FOOD BINGO!" See patterns on pages 165-168.

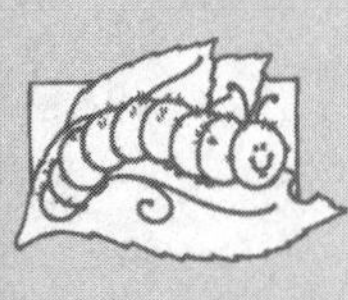
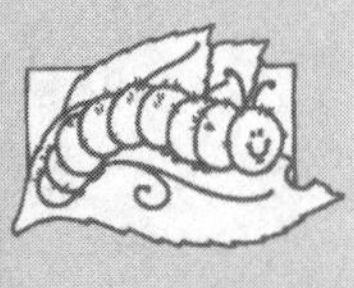
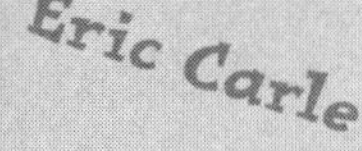

Arts/Crafts Experience

• Let students make move-able caterpillar puppets! All you need is colored cotton balls (found in craft stores), a couple of straws and a needle and thread. Thread the needle through seven or eight colored cotton balls to make the caterpillar body. After the first few cotton balls have been threaded, poke a hole through the top of a straw and thread the needle through it, also. If you thread through two straws with the cotton balls, they can be handles for your "marionette" so you can move it.

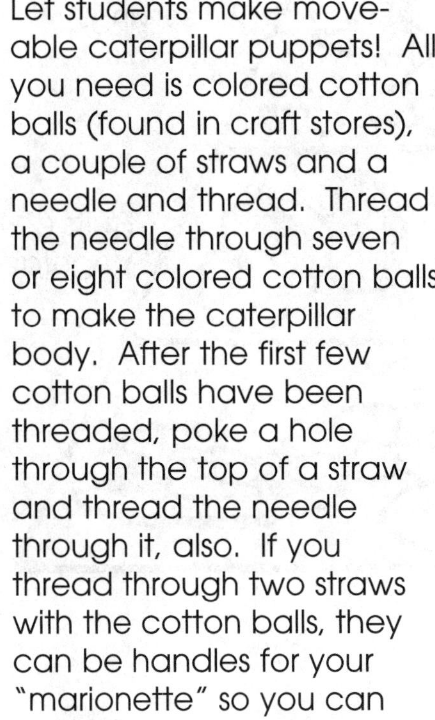

Arts/Crafts Experience continued

• Eric Carle's illustrations are made from a combination of tissue and paint. Let your students try a similar art technique. Have them take several pieces of colorful tissue paper torn into different shapes if desired and lay them on white art paper. They spray the paper with a spray bottle of water, then let it dry. After the tissue dries, they carefully lift off the tissue paper to reveal the design or picture underneath. They can add final details or features with crayons or markers.

• Students can create their own hungry caterpillars with green construction paper chain loops, adding features such as eyes, mouth and antennae on the first loop. Allow the students to paint segments of the Hungry Caterpillar's body in bright tempera colors. If the segments are large enough, they can be hung one segment at a time and then connected to the caterpillar head to hang from the ceiling. You could also hang some of the food he ate through. Very colorful and livens up a room!

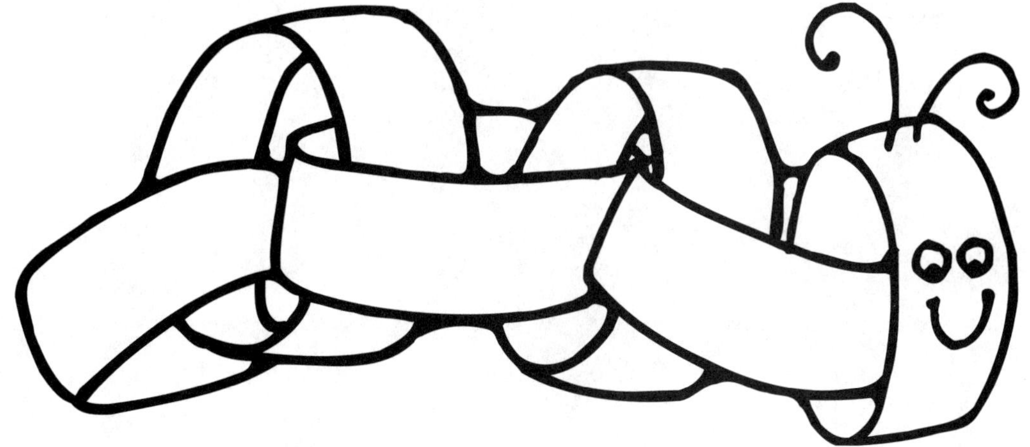

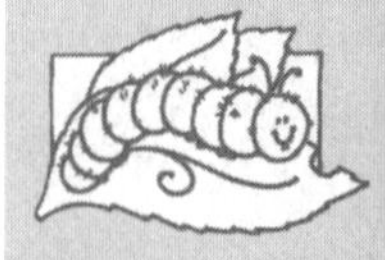

Extension Activities

- Invite adults from your school (custodian, nurse, principal, guidance counselor, etc.) to come and share their favorite Eric Carle books with your class.

- After reading *The Hungry Caterpillar* to your class, serve edible "caterpillars" (gummy worms) or the pieces of fruit illustrated in the story to your students.

- After reading *The Very Busy Spider* to your class, eat a not-so-busy spider! Provide students with a couple of round snack crackers. Students spread cheese spread between the two crackers for the spider body. Then they insert eight pretzel stick "spider legs" into the cheese spread all around the sides of its body. Finally, dip a couple of raisin "eyes" into cheese spread and mount them on the top of the cracker creation!

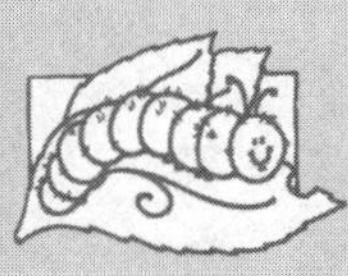

Follow-Up/Homework Idea

- Challenge students to search for live caterpillars, ladybugs and spiders in their yards (but not to harm them).

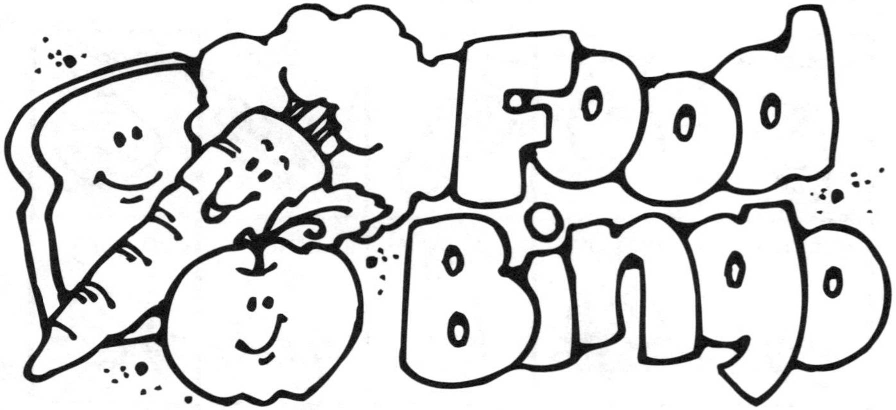

Food Bingo

Card 2

Cookie	Bacon	Lettuce	Steak	Butter
Bagel	Apple	Cheese	Pear	Cucumber
Milk	Eggs	FREE!	Onion	Orange
Banana	Cereal	Radish	Bread	Carrot
Cherries	Lemonade	Chicken	Potato	Soup

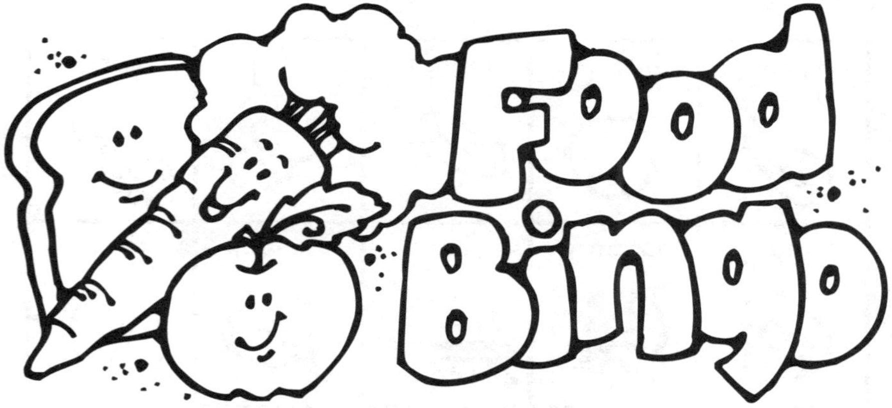

Food Bingo

Card 1

Pear	Lettuce	Cereal	Bagel	Chicken
Eggs	Carrot	Cheese	Apple	Onion
Bread	Bacon	FREE!	Potato	Steak
Orange	Radish	Soup	Milk	Cherries
Cucumber	Butter	Lemonade	Cookie	Banana

Food Bingo

Card 4

Bacon	Carrot	Cherries	Cookie	Chicken
Cucumber	Lemonade	Milk	Lettuce	Orange
Onion	Steak	FREE!	Soup	Butter
Cheese	Banana	Apple	Cereal	Eggs
Pear	Potato	Bread	Bagel	Radish

Food Bingo

Card 3

Butter	Soup	Banana	Radish	Lemonade
Eggs	Bread	Pear	Lettuce	Apple
Bagel	Carrot	FREE!	Milk	Cucumber
Potato	Cereal	Cheese	Steak	Bacon
Chicken	Cherries	Orange	Onion	Cookie

Food Bingo

Card 6

Cherries	Cheese	Soup	Radish	Cookie
Cereal	Pear	Lettuce	Chicken	Orange
Carrot	Bagel	FREE!	Potato	Apple
Eggs	Milk	Butter	Onion	Cucumber
Banana	Bacon	Steak	Bread	Lemonade

Food Bingo

Card 5

Onion	Lemonade	Bread	Soup	Milk
Potato	Cheese	Cereal	Banana	Eggs
Orange	Radish	FREE!	Bacon	Carrot
Chicken	Apple	Pear	Steak	Lettuce
Cookie	Bagel	Cucumber	Butter	Cherries

Food Bingo

Card 8

Milk	Cucumber	Potato	Cherries	Lettuce
Orange	Carrot	Radish	Cereal	Cookie
Bagel	Lemonade	FREE!	Banana	Soup
Onion	Bread	Bacon	Pear	Butter
Apple	Cheese	Chicken	Steak	Eggs

Food Bingo

Card 7

Pear	Cookie	Cheese	Eggs	Potato
Steak	Radish	Bagel	Butter	Cherries
Bread	Onion	FREE!	Lettuce	Carrot
Soup	Bacon	Apple	Chicken	Orange
Cereal	Cucumber	Lemonade	Milk	Banana

Pied Piper Day

June 26

Setting the Stage

- Display pictures of mice, toy mice and a big piece of cheese surrounded by related literature to gather interest in the day's theme.

- Construct a semantic web with words your students think of when you say the word *mouse*.

Historical Background

According to a popular legend of the Middle Ages, the Pied Piper of Hamelin rid a German town of its rat problem. When he discovered he was not going to be paid his reward of a sack of gold, he supposedly lured all the village children to a mountainside and they were never seen or heard of again.

Literary Exploration

Amos and Boris by William Steig
Anatole and the Pied Piper of Hamelin by Eve Titus
Another Mouse to Feed by Robert Krauss
A Cat and Mouse Story by Michael Rosen
Frederick by Leo Lionni
If You Give a Mouse a Cookie by Laura Joffe Numeroff
The Little Mouse, the Red Ripe Strawberry, and the Big Hungry Bear by
   Don and Audrey Wood
The Mice of Nibbling Village by Jane Pinkney
Mouse by Sara Stein
Mouse and the Motorcycle (series) by Beverly Cleary
Mouse Count by Ellen Stoll Walsh
Mouse Days: A Book of Season by Leo Lionni
Mousekin (series) by Edna Miller
Mouse Paint by Ellen Stoll Walsh
Mouse Soup by Arnold Lobel
Mouse Tales by Arnold Lobel
Mrs. Frisby and the Rats of NIMH by Robert O'Brien
Norman the Doorman by Don Freeman
Once a Mouse by Marcia Brown
The Pied Piper of Hamelin by Deborah Hautzig
The Pied Piper of Hamelin by Mercer Mayer
The Pied Piper of Hamelin by Tony Ross
The Pied Piper of Hamelin by Terry Small
The Town Mouse and the Country Mouse by Helen Craig
Where's Mouse? by Alan Baker
Whose Mouse Are You? by Robert Krauss

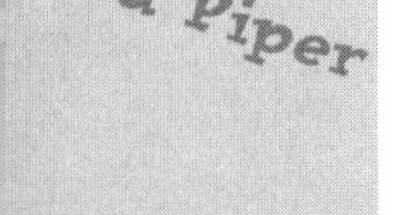

Science/Health Experience

• Learn about rats and their habitats.

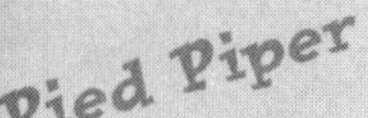

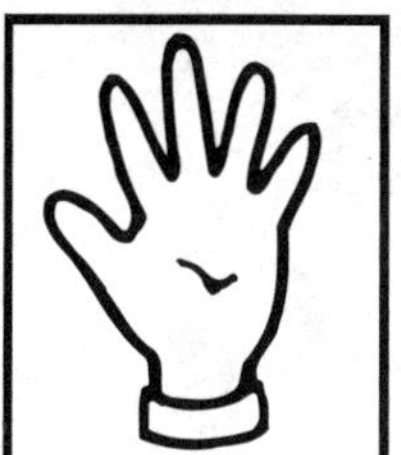

Physical/Sensory Experience
• Play a tag game of Cat and Mouse!

Arts/Crafts Experience
• Students can make cute furry little mice out of gray felt pieces, with a small pink pom-pom nose, wiggly eyes and a pipe cleaner tail.

Extension Activities
⚠ Serve cheese crackers and an Edible Mouse! Use a canned pear "body," a cherry "nose," two raisin "eyes," two almond sliver "ears," small pieces of uncooked spaghetti "whiskers" and a thin piece of licorice for a tail.

⚠ Cut an end piece of banana (dipping it in lemon juice to prevent browning), then add features the same as on the pear mouse.

Follow-Up/Homework Idea
• Encourage students to be as quiet as mice while they read at home.

Helen Keller's Birthday

June 27

Setting the Stage

- Display books about various people who have dealt with handicaps, living extraordinary lives, including Helen Keller.

- Braille is a system of raised dots to represent letters of the alphabet. Blind people can read by touching the raised dots. Try to have some Braille books for students to look through and feel.

Historical Background

American author, educator and lecturer, Helen Keller, was born on this day in 1880. A movie, *The Miracle Worker*, was made about how she learned to communicate in spite of her inability to see or hear.

Literary Exploration

Amy: The Story of a Deaf Child by LouAnn Walker
The Eye and Seeing by Brian Ward
My Five Senses by Margret Miller
Helen Keller by Margaret Davidson
Helen Keller by Stewart and Polly Anne Graff
Helen Keller by Nigel Hunter
Helen Keller by Richard Tames
Helen Keller by Dennis Wepman
Helen Keller's Teacher by Margaret Davidson
The Helen Keller Story by Catherine Owens Peare
I Have a Sister, My Sister Is Deaf by Jeanne Whitehouse Peterson
Louis Braille: The Boy Who Invented Books for the Blind by Margaret
    Davidson
A Picture Book of Helen Keller by David A. Adler
The Story of Annie Sullivan: Helen Keller's Teacher by Bernice Selden
The Story of My Life by Helen Keller
The Value of Determination: The Story of Helen Keller by Ann Donegan
    Johnson

Writing Experience

• Bring an encyclopedia with a Braille alphabet in it and make a copy
  for every student. Have students write their names in Braille. They can
  use a pencil to press the letters through the back of the paper creat-
  ing a raised surface.

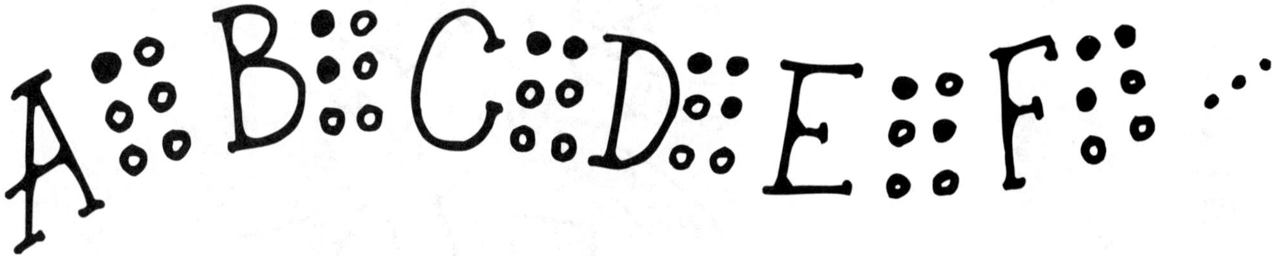

• Students can write about one of the following topics:

> It's hard for me to . . .
> If I were blind . . .
> I'd like to see . . .

Math Experience

• Borrow an eye chart from the school nurse's office or from a local optometrist. Let students practice using hand directions (on the chart) from various distances in the room. Then they can measure the distances at which they can see the different rows of letters.

Science/Health Experience

• Review the five senses and how they help us discover the world around us.

Social Studies Experience

• Learn about the life and contributions of Helen Keller and her teacher Annie Sullivan.

Music/Dramatic Experience

• Annie Sullivan Macy was the teacher who taught Helen Keller by spelling words with her fingers in Helen's hands. Let students practice this with partners. They can re-enact what those moments may have been like when Helen Keller realized she could communicate with her teacher.

Physical/Sensory Experience

• Play Blind Man's Bluff. Blindfold one player and have him or her try to tag other players in a certain area. The other players try to keep very still, out of his or her way. The last person caught becomes the next "Blind Man."

• Simulate a "being blind" experience for your students by pairing them up and letting one lead the other blindfolded around the playground. The "sighted" student must be careful to lead around or away from any obstacles. They can switch positions and later talk about how it felt having to trust their partner.

• Learn some basic sign language such as, "I love you!"

Arts/Crafts Experience

- Pair up students and blindfold one while the other person gives directions for an art project. The blindfolded students try to follow the directions exactly. Then have them switch roles. Afterwards, they can compare their art project results.

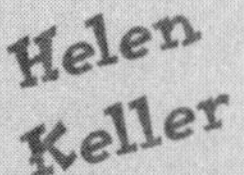

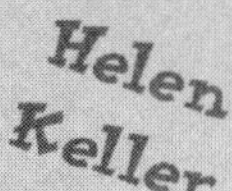

Extension Activities

- Invite a person who has dealt with a physical handicap to come and speak to your class about overcoming challenges.

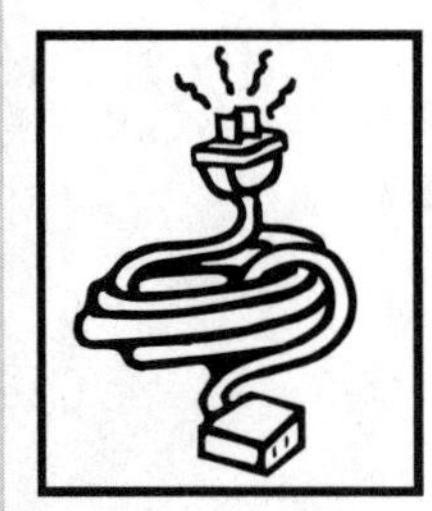

Values Education Experience

- Discuss what Helen Keller may have meant when she said, "We can do anything we want to if we stick to it long enough." Discuss persistence.

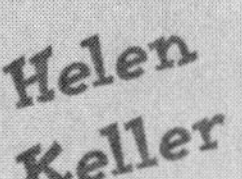

Follow-Up/Homework Idea

- Encourage students to go home and look at the world as if seeing everything for the first time.

At the Beach Day

June 28

Setting the Stage

- Display beach paraphernalia (pails and shovels, towels, sunscreen, beach chair, umbrella, inflatable beach toys, etc.) with related literature to gather excitement in today's activities. Fill a wading pool with books about the beach.

- Create a bulletin board with sandpaper to represent sand on the beach. Add seashells and ocean pictures. Use blue butcher paper, tissue paper or cellophane to represent the waves of the ocean.

- Construct a semantic web with facts your students know about the beach. Then list questions they want answered today.

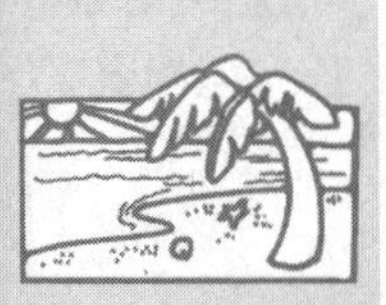

Literary Exploration

Abigal at the Beach by Felix Pirani
Are We Almost There? by James Stevenson
The Art and Industry of Sandcastles by Jan Adkins
At the Beach by Huy Voun Lee
At the Beach by Anne Rockwell
Beach Ball by Peter Sis
The Beach Before Breakfast by M.W. Kumin
Beachcomber's Book by Bernice Kohn
A Beach Day by Douglas Florian
Beach Days by Ken Robbins
Blue Bug's Beach Party by Virginia Poulet
The Castle Builder by Dennis Nolan
Curious George at the Beach by Margret Rey
Day at the Beach by Mircea Vasiliu
Down to the Beach by May Garelick
Emma at the Beach by James Stevenson
Let's Go to the Beach by Harriet Huntington
Little Bunny at the Beach by Ulf Nilsson
Morning Beach by Leslie Baker
On My Beach There Are Many Pebbles by Leo Lionni
Sand Castle by Ronald Wegen
Sea and Seashore by Terry Jennings
The Sea Is Calling Me by Lee Bennett Hopkins
Seashore by Steve Parker
The Seashore Book by E. Boyd Smith
Seashores by Joyce Pope
Seashores by Herbert S. Zim and Lester Ingle
Snoopy's Facts and Fun Book About Seashores by Charles M. Schulz
The Summerfolk by Doris Burn
Tom and Pippo at the Beach by Helen Oxenbury
Where the Waves Break: Life at the Edge of the Sea by Anita Malnig

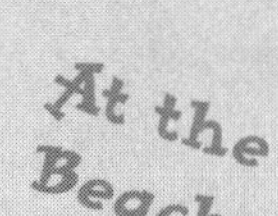
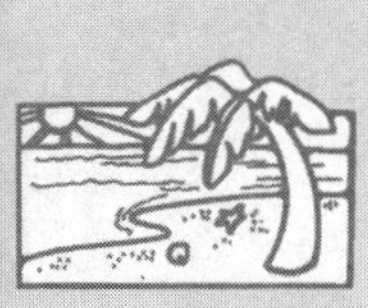

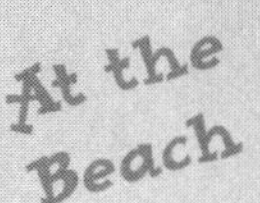

Language Experience

• Encourage students (ahead of time) to bring beach towels or lawn chairs and sunglasses so they can each settle down with a good book.

Math Experience

- Bring real sand to play Beach Blanket Bingo in the sand. Give review math questions and have students look for appropriate answers. Let students write a number in each square, then instead of covering up a square at the right answer, they erase it in the sand!

Science/Health Experience

- Review beach and water safety.

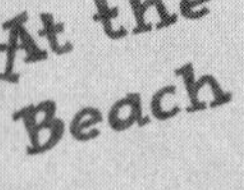

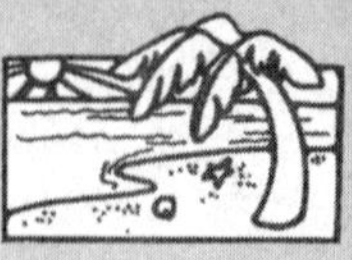

Social Studies Experience

- Have students locate areas around the world that host great beach sites (such as the Florida and California coasts).

Music/Dramatic Experience

- Play Beach Boys music while students work on their projects.

- Play a recording of seashore sounds—ocean waves, birds, etc., and have students pretend they're sunbathing at the beach.

Physical/Sensory Experience

- Let students make their own sand! Explain that sand was once part of larger rocks. Ocean waves, freezing water and weather such as rain and wind, erode rocks and leave fragments. Give each student two rocks and a piece of paper. Have them rub the rocks together and compare the sandy granules that drop onto the paper with sand from the beach.

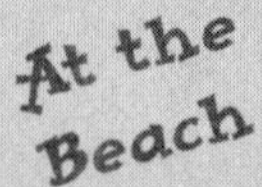

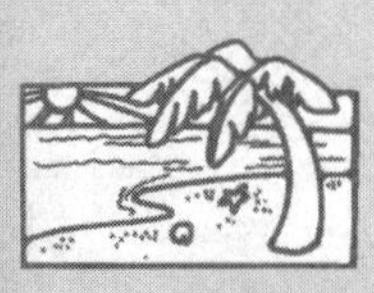

Physical/Sensory Experience continued

• Bring a shell collection and let students group the shells according to color, shape and size.

• Play a simplified version of sand volleyball with a beach ball!

Arts/Crafts Experience

• If you have access to a sand play area for young children, let your students build sand castles and create other works of art. If a sand area is not available, create your own by filling up a small inflatable swimming pool with sand from a local garden center. To make the sand castles last a little longer, add a mixture of one part water and one part cornstarch to two parts sand. Students can invert sand pails and plastic cups for a basic formation, then add interesting details with odds and ends they find.

• Students can make textured starfish! Have each one draw a starfish shape on yellow construction paper or tag board, then brush a coat of glue over it. Then crumble Shredded Wheat Cereal™ and spread it evenly on the starfish.

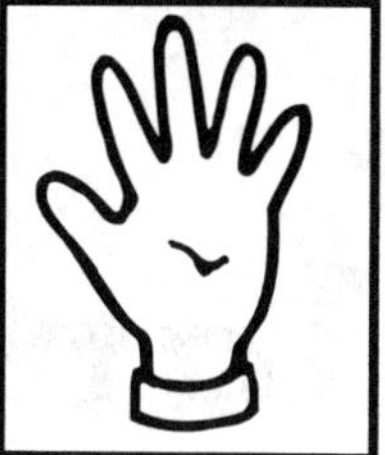

Physical/Sensory Experience continued

- Students can make art projects in-the-round! Have each bring a clean jar or can from home. Provide sandpaper to wrap around the can or jar and attach it with rubber cement. (Waiting a minute or two before actually sticking it to the jar will make it stick better.) Students can glue or draw beach details (seashells, crabs, etc.) on the sand all the way around the can or jar.

Extension Activities

⚠ Fill a wading pool with ice and cold drinks for a summery treat!

⚠ Serve starfish tuna sandwiches! Students can shape their bread slices into starfish and scoop a mound of tuna between the layers. Dipping olives in mayonnaise or cream cheese can make starfish eyes.

Follow-Up/Homework Idea

- Students can share memories of fun trips to the beach or plan one in the future with their families.

Sports Spectacular Day

June 29

Setting the Stage

- Display various types of sports equipment (bats, balls, helmets, rackets) around related literature.

- Construct a semantic web with facts your students know (or would like to know) about sports.

Historical Background

On this day in 1880, a woman completed a 1000-mile walk in 1000 hours. Charles Dumas jumped seven feet in the high jump in 1956. In 1985 Bob Brown set a record with his yo-yo for over 120 hours of continuous movement. Just a few of the many great days in sports history!

Literary Exploration

Baseball, Football, Daddy, and Me by David Friend
The Giant Book of More Strange but True Sports Stories by Howard Liss
How Sports Came to Be by Don L. Wulffson

Language Experience

• Let students brainstorm as many kinds of sports as they can. List them on the board and let them try to alphabetize the list.

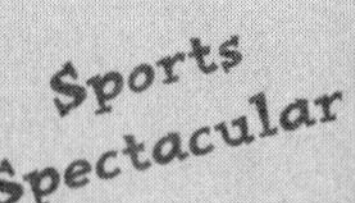

Writing Experience

• Encourage students to dream up new sports! Have them write the rules, instructions, area needed, number of players as well as any equipment needed to play. See reproducible on page 186.

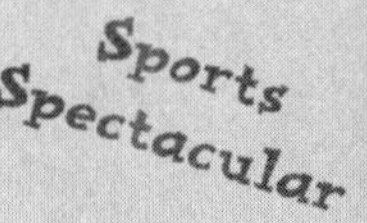

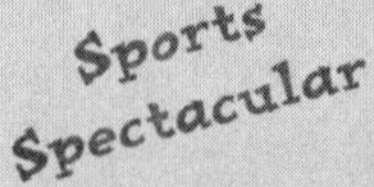

Math Experience

• Let students survey one another about their favorite sports and add the information to a class bar graph.

Science/Health Experience
• Review sports safety.

Social Studies Experience
• Share historical highlights from *How Sports Came to Be* by Don L. Wulffson.

• Study sports popular in other countries.

Music/Dramatic Experience
• Plays Sports Charade! Let students pantomime various sports for the rest of the class to guess.

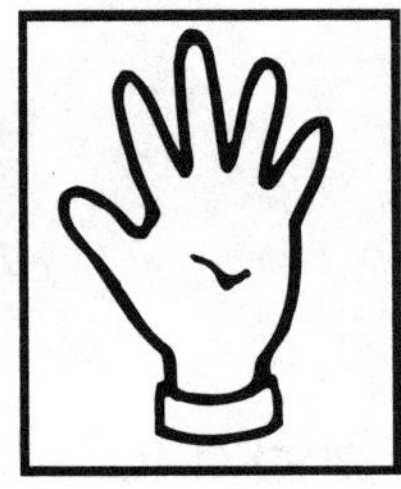

Physical/Sensory Experience
• Host a Sports Marathon letting students play as many sports as will fit in with your curriculum day.

Arts/Crafts Experience

• Let students draw pictures of themselves, playing their favorite sports.

Extension Activities

• If possible, take your class to a local high school sports event as a field trip.

• Invite a local junior high or high school athlete to visit your class and tell why he or she likes being involved in sports.

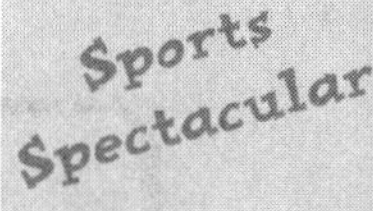

Values Education Experience

• Discuss what it means to be a team player and to demonstrate good sportsmanship. Ask students to share their ideas about what *good sportsmanship* means (following the rules, not accusing others of cheating, etc.).

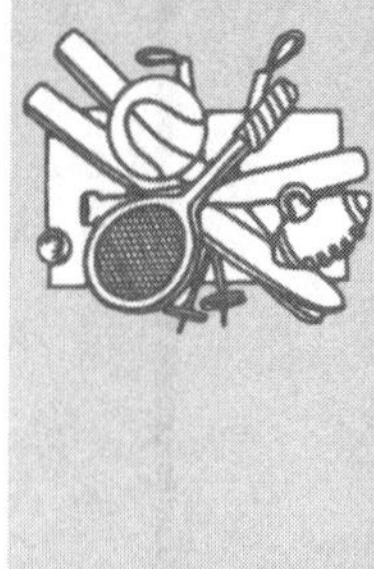

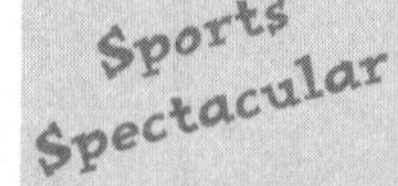

Follow-Up/Homework Idea

• Students can go home and play sports with their family members or neighborhood friends.

It's
a
new
SPORT!

Half-Year Birthday

June 30

Setting the Stage

- Display birthday paraphernalia (streamers, confetti, balloons, etc.) surrounded by related literature to get your students excited about today's activities.

- Construct a semantic web with words your students think of when you say *birthday*.

Literary Exploration

Arthur's Birthday by Marc Brown
Confetti by Phyllis Fiarotta
The Golden Happy Birthday Book by Barbara Shook Hazen
Half a Button by Lyn Hoopes
Half a Kingdom by Ann McGovern
Half a Moon and One Whole Star by Crescent Dragonwagon
The Half-Birthday Party by Charlotte Pomerantz
Half for You by Meyer Azaad
Happy Birthday to Me by Anne and Harlow Rockwell
Jenny's Birthday by Esther Holden Averill
Less Than Half, More Than Whole by Kathleen Lacapa
The One Bad Thing About Birthdays by David Collins
Surprise Birthday by Anabelle Prager

Language Experience

• Let students read half a story in a book, then draw their own conclusions about how the story ends.

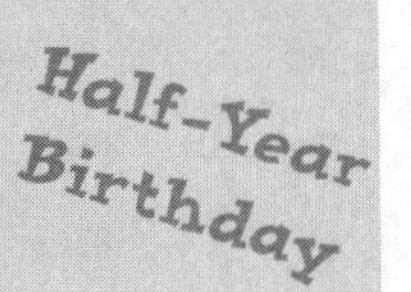

Writing Experience

• Students can write about an unusual birthday or how they would feel if everyone forgot their birthday. See reproducible on page 191.

• Have students write poems to wish other a half year birthday.

Math Experience

- Let students pick which half of their math problems they want to do today.

- Challenge students to figure out how old they are by years, months, weeks and days.

Science/Health Experience

- Review with your students what they have learned in science and health during the first half of the year.

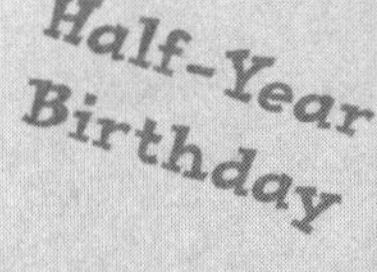

Music/Dramatic Experience

- Students will enjoy working in pairs to act out funny skits where each one is half a person. (Example: One student puts his arms behind his back. His partner sticks his arms in front of the other person and acts as his arms to gesture, draw, write, etc.)

Physical/Sensory Experience

- Have a half-shoe relay! Divide students into teams. They take turns running to one end of the playing field where they drop off a shoe, run back to the starting position, run once more to take off the other shoe and run back to the line. They do this for the first round, then for the second round they run to the designated area and put on a shoe at each round. It gets tricky when they have to find one shoe at a time with everyone else's shoe there, also.

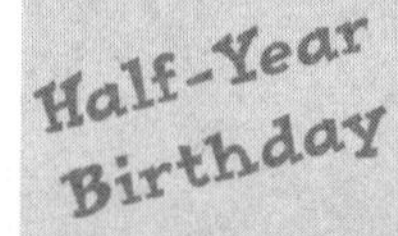

Arts/Crafts Experience

• Review the art principle of symmetry. Let students finish the other half of an art project or picture.

Extension Activities

⚠ Make just a half a cake and serve everyone half a piece! Give each student half a glass of lemonade to go with it.

Follow-Up/Homework Idea

• Encourage your students to make the second half of the year even better than the first!

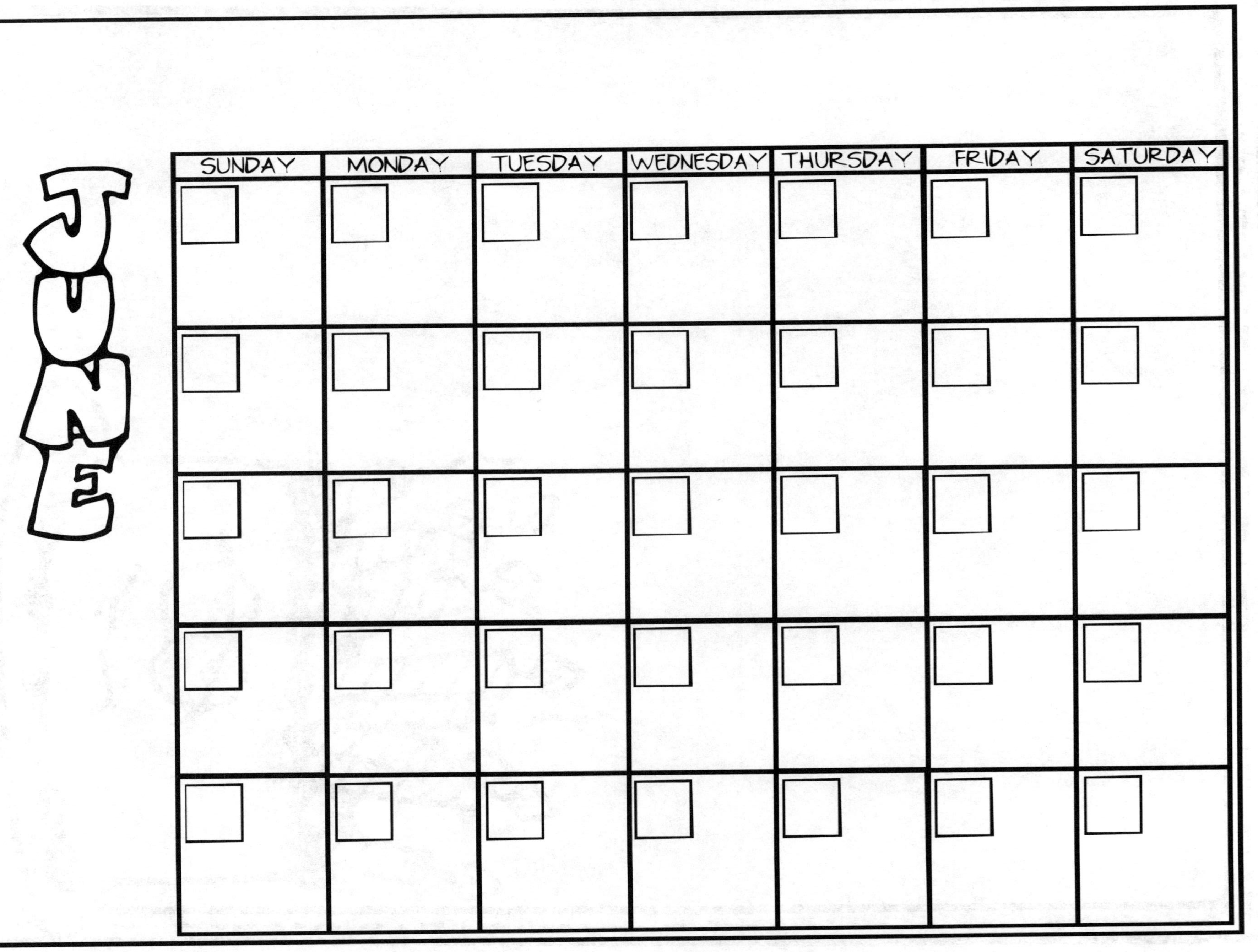

JUNE
SUNDAY
MONDAY
TUESDAY
WEDNESDAY
THURSDAY
FRIDAY
SATURDAY